LOST & FOUND

"You can't help but be inspired by Paul's epic and wild adventures. It is a gripping yarn that details the awe-inspiring achievements of a humble Australian who has taken on and conquered surely one of the toughest adventures on this planet. This should be compulsory reading for those wanting to understand themselves and how to break through self imposed limitations."

Peter Baines OAM
Founder & Director of International Operations
Hands Group

"Paul is one of those people that makes you believe that 'you can do it too.' He has no 'special qualities' or 'superpowers', just an ordinary guy with drive, determination and guts.
His story shows us all that great adventures are well within our reach and all we have to do is try.

This book will have you laughing, crying and believing you can live a bigger life than you've ever imagined,
you just need to say yes."

Jane Erbacher
Founder ergarmy.com
@lululemonausnz Ambassador

Published by Paul Watkins, 2021
PO Box 5017 Warrnambool Vic 3280

Copyright © Paul Watkins, 2021

All rights reserved. Except as permitted under the Copyright Act 1968, (for example, a fair dealing for the purposes of study, research, criticism or review) no part of this book may be reproduced, stored in a retrieval system, or transmitted in any form or by any means without prior written permission from Paul Watkins. For further information, see www.roguescholar.com.au

Every effort has been made to trace and acknowledge copyright. However, should any infringement have occurred the publishers tender their apologies and invite copyright owners to contact them.

Cover design by Paul Watkins
Map Illustrations by Owen Delaney
Edited by Lu Sexton
Printed by Ingram Spark

Watkins, Paul   Lost and Found, why we need adventure
ISBN print - 978-0-6451444-0-6
ISBN ebook - 978-0-6451444-1-3

Disclaimer

The material in this publication is of the nature of general comment only and does not represent professional advice. It is not intended to provide specific guidance for any particular circumstances and it should not be relied upon for any decision to take action or not to take action on any matter which it covers. Readers should obtain professional advice where appropriate, before making any such decision. To the maximum extent permitted by law, the author and publisher disclaim all responsibility and liability to any person, arising directly or indirectly from any person taking or not taking action based on the information in this book.

LOST & FOUND

why we need adventure

PAUL WATKINS

For my wife
Ilona, for having the courage to marry her own life-size Harry Potter action figure.

For our boys
Campbell & Noah, for teaching me that my greatest and most important adventure is being their **Dad**

For my parents
Dad for his adventurous spirit, work ethic and loyalty.
Mum for teaching me to be cautious and sensible and tolerating my constant and flagrant disregard for both ideals.

For my brother
Scott and his sage like advice before every expedition, 'Remember, no hero shit'.

The weary mind

All events and conversations from both my adventures in the Arctic are recalled from the recesses of a memory that was starved of both sleep and food. Not to mention being frozen – but they are my honest recollections. Any errors are mine and mine alone.

Do you fear the wind?

Do you fear the force of the wind,
The slash of the rain?
Go face them and fight them,
Be savage again.
Go hungry and cold like the wolf,
Go wade like the crane:
The palms of your hands will thicken,
The skin of your cheek will tan,
You'll grow ragged and weary and swarthy,
 But you'll walk like a man.

From *The Trail of the Goldseekers,* 1895, by Hamlin Garland

About the author

As a professional, Paul brings his tales of adventure from the farthest reaches of the planet to schools, business, board rooms and conference centres. His stories are told with honesty, humour and the brutal realism that comes from someone trying to find his next adventure while also packing school lunches and dealing with the critical mass of laundry that comes from two young sons who love playing outside plus enough running and training gear to sink a battleship.

When he's not regaling people, Paul can be found tending dogs, chickens and cows on his piece of paradise in south-west Victoria. He divides his time between being a stay-at-home Dad, writing and blogging, managing investments, and getting time out running on the trails.

You can find him at www.paulwatkins.com.au .

Contents

A note from the author		xiii
Prologue	They are coming	1

Part one
The Quest to be Savage
(pre 6633 Arctic Ultra)

Chapter 1	Why be a savage?	7
Chapter 2	How did I get here?	13

Lessons

Lesson 1	The Stories we tell ourselves	33
Lesson 2	You are not your job.	49
Lesson 3	Go	57

Part two
The Toughest Race
(first attempt at 6633 Arctic Ultra)

Chapter 3	The 13 toughest races in the world	63
Chapter 4	Rise & grind	67
Chapter 5	Only 14,000km to go	79
Chapter 6	All roads lead to Fort Mac	89
Chapter 7	I'm not OK with this	103
Chapter 8	The decision	113
Chapter 9	Do. The. Work.	119
Chapter 10	Ladies and gentlemen – it's time	129

Lessons

Lesson 4	Take the hard road	143
Lesson 5	Roll with the punches	155
Lesson 6	The mind makes it real	165

Part three
Go Hungry & Cold like the Wolf
(second attempt at 6633 Arctic Ultra)

Chapter 11	Arctic Circle	179
Chapter 12	James Creek	183
Chapter 13	Fort McPherson	189
Chapter 14	Mid River	197
Chapter 15	Aklavik	203
Chapter 16	Inuvik	211
Chapter 17	Gateway	229
Chapter 18	Tuktoyaktuk	243
Chapter 19	Full circle	257
Epilogue	Do you fear the wind?	267
Post Script	What Happened Next	273

A note from the author

This book isn't a ten-step plan, or a map of self-help how-to. It is simply a real story. A true and honest account of how a nerdy Dad from a country town won one of the toughest races in the world. There are no superheroes, last minute miracles or divine intervention. There is failure, setbacks, self-doubt, sacrifice and reflection. And that's what makes it so valuable. This isn't about an Olympian or an astronaut or a superhero – it's about a person, someone a lot like you. A husband, a father, a son – with a job, responsibilities, emotions and doubts.

I believe that deep within all of us there lies a powerful undercurrent, a deep ocean on the move, slowly gathering pace over millennia, generation after generation. Whispering, calling, hinting at a life where we have ventured forth into adventure and challenge and wilderness – be it on a mountain side, the business world or just the intimate boundaries of our own immediate lives.

There are those who not only hear that whisper but also are adept at answering it – those who seem to have limitless reserves, confidence of self and an almost unshakeable belief that not only is there more to their story but that they will go and seek it out. This book is not for them.

There are those of us who can just hear the whisper, the quiet voice distilled somewhere in the back of our mind, the fringes of our psyche. We can hear and we know that there is more, more to our story, more to our lives – but that bridge, that door, the keys – all feel elusive. How to unlock the seal that separates us from the self that seems trapped in our 'modern life' but desperately needs to throw off some shackles and be 'more'. The dreamers, the hopeful, those hungry for more – this book is for you.

Lastly there are those for whom that quiet inner voice has been completely drowned out – through choice or circumstance. For them there is only the war within, a lost savage trapped in a modern frame, enveloped in a world that doesn't celebrate either. I hope this book opens some doors for them to escape and explore.

Either way – thank you for taking the time to pick this up, in a world where time and attention is in short supply I appreciate you consciously spending some of yours here.

This book is both a rollicking tale of adventure in the Arctic as well as a reflection on the lessons learned – from the highs and the lows – and how you can take those lessons and apply them to your own life. Right now. And maybe, find the bridge that spans the chasm between where you are and where you want to be.

I've divided this book into two themes – for both my sanity and to make it easier for you to navigate – 'the story' and 'the lessons'. I know – stunningly original nomenclature, but it serves to keep us all on track. It's presented in blocks so that you can easily separate the two.

You can just dive in and enjoy the tale and then come back to lessons and strategies separately down the track, or you can roll straight from start to finish and see the entire evolution. Either way, I hope you enjoy the ride and ind some value and tools that inspire you to tune into that voice inside. I sincerely hope that it sparks a great adventure for you – whatever that may be, because that's where all the best stories hide.

The very best stories are your own.
But in the interim, here's mine.

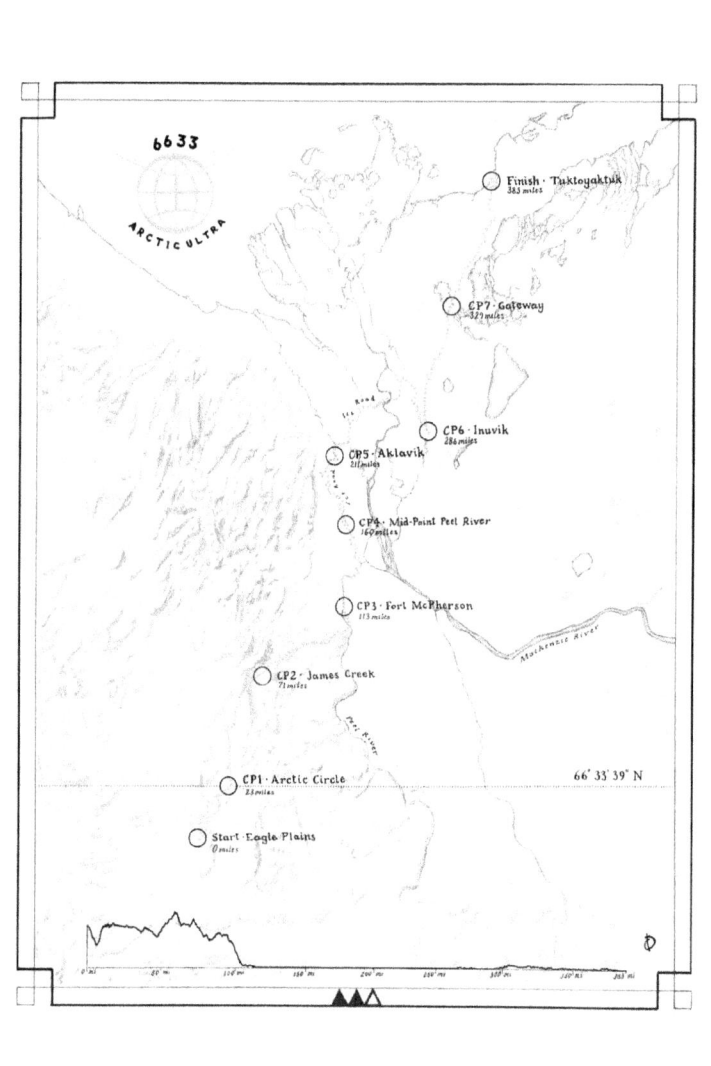

PROLOGUE

They are coming

Northwest Territories, Canada
6633 Arctic Ultra 2019
Thursday 14 March, 2019, approx 5:30am
Distance from start line – 491km
Distance to finish line – 123 m
Time racing – 6 days, 14 hours, 3 minutes.

I KNOW THEY ARE COMING.
   The chase pack.
   The Irishman, the Romanian and the American.
   It took me four days to catch them and two days to put some distance between us. I've fought for every kilometre. I have been racing for almost 160 hours, with probably another 30 hours between me and the inish line. Over the last six days I have managed a total of roughly 12 hours of sleep – most of that in a bivvy bag on the ice and snow.
   I know they are coming.

The Romanian, Avram, is literally singing his way along the ice road. He's all smiles, but you don't swim the 2,860km length of the Danube without a wetsuit, surviving on happy thoughts and showtunes alone. He must have lungs like mighty blacksmith bellows, capable of stoking some fierce athletic fire within.

The American, David, is a jack of all trades – preacher, attorney, heavy machine operator. The time we spent together earlier on the trail left me with the impression that he was not just thoughtful but practical, with a propensity for action, not hesitation. The freezing cold of Montana didn't crack him so I know the weather here won't either.

I've never met a soft Irishman and Patrick is no exception. He's all smiles and lyrical Irish lilt, but underneath there's a tough-as-nails athlete. He's driven; he's been here before. He's run down everyone else, there's only me left. He's just there, I can feel it.

They know where I am, I have no idea where they are. Just behind the last hill? Five kilometres back? Ten? They can see my every move – depicted crisply in the track I leave in the snow. Stop to sleep, eat, answer a call of nature – all broadcast in the pressed white narrative at my feet. They know my every move. I trudge and push my exhausted frame forward into the fresh cover of light snow and crushed rock. I remind myself, 'Don't look back. Don't look back. All that matters is what you do.'

Find the problem, fix the problem. The finish line is about 120km away, with this load and these conditions that's about 30 hours of hard graft. Keep moving no matter what, hold the line, push the pace.

I thought that was my only problem, but deep within a much

bigger contest was at play. You can be as mentally strong as you like but sooner or later chemistry always wins. Six and half days of brutal sleep deprivation had been slowly but surely pounding my hypothalamus, deep within my brain, into willful submission. The delicate dance of neuro-chemicals had slowly but surely descended into chaos, the normally carefully curated cocktail that commands whether we are asleep or awake was about to violently veer off course.

I know they are coming.

Push the pace.

You must keep moving.

It was my last thought as I blacked out, my depleted body collapsed and I hit the ground.

They are coming.

And I have stopped.

(Continued in Part Three – Go Hungry & Cold like the Wolf)

part one

THE QUEST TO BE SAVAGE (PRE 6633 ARCTIC ULTRA)

CHAPTER 1

Why be a savage?

'Do you fear the force of the wind, the slash of the rain
Go face them and fight them,
Be savage again'

Hamlin Garland, 1895

WHEN YOU SPEND ALMOST 200 HOURS walking across the frozen Arctic tundra, pretty much completely alone, you find yourself with plenty of time to think. Sometimes it's about mission critical stuff – have I eaten enough, how's my pacing, when did I drink last? Sometimes it's about not so mission critical matters – 'Pantaloons, Pantaloons, Pantaloons, Pantaloons…confirmed, funniest word in the English language.' Seriously, try saying that word over and over, it sticks and gets funnier every time. Or maybe that's just the cumulative toll of days of sleep deprivation and extreme isolation. Either way – I found it hilarious at the time. And then, just occasionally, you ponder something of actual significance, 'What if we have lost the art of being savage?'

'BE SAVAGE AGAIN...'

It's a theory that has been rolling around in my brain pan for some time now – I have no empirical evidence, no nuanced data set to back up my claim – at least not yet. Just a nagging sensation in the back of my brain that rears its head whenever I'm on an expedition or facing the elements in a race like the 6633 Arctic Ultra. As a man o 43 years o age, I'm still figuring my way out in the world, how to balance being a husband, a father, a friend and most of all – just me. And raising my two boys makes it even more complex – where is the guidebook for helping my young boys develop resilience and fortitude while balancing empathy and sensitivity? How can I mould for them a path that gives them the chance to be both noble yet rugged, the warrior and the poet? Set the kiln too hot and you set brittle the clay, too cool and leave it unhardened.

Society is rocketing forward to a far more cerebral future – and rightly so. The days of needing the rugged frontiersman, the hunter/gatherer have all but passed. It's the speed with which we have moved forward that has caught us out. Sure I'm good with the latest gadgets, I can harness the power of the internet and use all modern medicine has to offer to the betterment of me and mine, but there still lies deep within the recesses of my brain – the primordial lizard component that was shaped by millennia and will not be spliced away so quickly – a need to reaffirm that the savage is still there. That I still have the capacity to face the force of the wind and slash of the rain, as the poet Hamlin Garland so eloquently put it.

Whenever I do Q&A at presentations or seminars, there are two guaranteed questions from the audience. First – where/how do you go to the toilet when it's -37C, blowing a gale and you're in the middle of Antarctica? The answer – with extreme efficiency and accuracy. The second question is shorter and far more complex – why? Not why do you go to the toilet when it's -37C, but why put yourself through all this hardship when you could just stay at home, watch something on NatGeo and live vicariously instead?

There is always the flippant answer to the question of 'why', nonchalantly thrown around, particularly in mountaineering circles – 'I climbed it because it was there'. Such a dismissive answer does a disservice to the deep personal sacrifices, months or years of dedication required to see these adventures to their conclusion. It disrespects those who may have tried and failed – often through no fault of their own. Lastly it devalues the importance of why we need to have these adventures in the first place. That seemingly inexplicable need to throw ourselves out of our comfort zone and test the mettle. All those that venture forth beyond safe and 'normal' boundaries will have their own answer, but perhaps deep down they are all just variations on a theme. An undercurrent driving us to seek out our own form of adventure – some of us are perhaps better at hearing that call and answering it. Perhaps others hear it but are unsure how to answer, finding themselves at war with a need to reconcile the savage within with the civilised world without. Others may have lost the ability to hear the call at all, it's been drowned out, willingly or unwillingly, by the harpy cry of modernity, finding themselves trapped between two irreconcilables, a caged animal.

The challenge therefore lies in hearing that low guttural tone from deep within and understanding not only what it means, but how to set it free from time to time in a manner that builds, not destroys. To let loose the lost savage within to drive ourselves to have the story that we quietly, even unconsciously, yearn for. The desire to be more.

'GO FACE THEM AND FIGHT THEM…'

Victory, dominance, the all-conquering hero. Everyone wants to be a winner but over who and what?

Let's get some context – I'm not an athlete, certainly not by design. I'm a nerd who ended up climbing big mountains and racing across the planet firstly as an escape and finally as a means to an end. It sets me free, recharges my savage batteries and reminds me that I am capable of raw and powerful behaviour – but one that doesn't correspond to violence or domination of others.

My opponent, for want of a better term, is both the elements, the environment and the battle that rages within to stay disciplined, to dig to the bottom of the well and then to keep digging. It's hardship but it's a 'healthy hardship' as Ross Edgeley puts it. My nerdy side enjoys the planning, the logistics, the strategy of coming to an expedition or race – ready to do battle. Once we are on the trail, the savage knows he will be called upon to rail against all before and within. I know that towards the final days of the 6633 Arctic Ultra, when the unrelenting cold was striving to crack me and countless days of sleep deprivation was crushing, every muscle and bone aching – I had to go to that dark room, deep inside and let out whatever lived there. Give over to anger and rage and sheer will to drive my worn and weary body forward. I didn't care if it broke or splintered or cried for help – the savage was out and there would be only one of two acceptable outcomes – complete victory or utter destruction. I'm not talking about the kind of anger that sees fists flying – it's a quiet, seething boil that I could direct and focus on whatever I needed. It was personal and powerful yet it left no one marked or scarred. And when I crossed the finish line, it was no longer needed and could be left to return to its dark corner – satiated and ready to slumber until needed once more.

These kinds of hardships will give you the chance to tap into that savage and use it in a way that benefits all and harms none. I fear that too often we misunderstand that guttural voice and think it needs to dominate others, through violence, subjugation or intimidation. In reality, I believe that the answer lies in needing to conquer ourselves, or our circumstances, or the elements – the elements particularly present both an eternal and timeless challenge that we still respond to in the most base and raw of terms. I like the term 'healthy hardship' as it sets this apart from the unwanted hardship of loss, trauma or catastrophe, but speaks more of challenge and trial that can accommodate both failure or success but still leave us whole and ready to fight another day.

It doesn't have to be some epic adventure into the frozen Arctic.

It can be as simple as conquering the marathon you always wanted to do, the call of the mountains, the weekend on the trail.

Can you last a week in the woods, will you compete in the ring? Will you set off not knowing the outcome but face it and fight it anyway?

> 'The force of the wind, slash of the rain
> Go face them and fight them...'

CHAPTER 2
How did I get here?

Victoria, Australia
1996–2017

HOW DOES A NERDY, MIDDLE AGED Dad from a regional country town, with no athletic pedigree or accolades, end up dragging a sled across the Arctic in a race of truly epic proportions? In some ways this could've easily been the shortest chapter in the book. How did we get here? No idea. Literally, that's it. How the hell did a skinny kid, strong on the academic scale, non-existent on the sporting scale, go from the debating team and Dungeons and Dragons, to building an impressive resume of mountain climbs, wild adventures and epic races in some of the most remote and unforgiving parts of the planet. The most accurate answer would be, I have no idea.

In some ways it would be far more helpful if I could tell you it was all part of a grand plan, carefully thought out and structured, executed with precision and that you too, dear reader, can follow these ten simple steps to become an adventurer par excellence in a matter of only a few short decades. Alas there is no ten-step plan, no carefully laid out strategy – there is only real life. Missteps, failures, setbacks, coincidences, gambles taken, opportunities lost and hearts followed. In amongst all of that there is definitely lessons to be gleaned, so let's delve a little into my nerdy past and set out a rough sketch of how I went from the comforts of academia in Melbourne, Australia to dragging a sled to the very end of Canada, literally standing on the frozen Arctic Ocean wondering if at any moment I would wake up and it would all be a dream.

THE BEST LAID PLANS

When I started my final year of high school I was well and truly convinced that I had the next major steps of my life clearly planned out. I had earned an academic scholarship to a private boys school in Melbourne, a scholarship which, along with the considerable sacrifices of my parents, allowed me to attend a school that would have otherwise been well and truly out of reach. It was traditionalist in every sense – the principal had a fulltime residence on campus, we had compulsory Army Cadet training for a minimum of four of our six years there, and the school marshal was pretty handy with the cane if discipline was required. After-school sport was compulsory – all other extra-curriculum pursuits such as debating or theatre – were very much optional. For a school that was very proud of its academic achievements (which is generally the most important yardstick for parents) it seemed, to me at least, to place an undue amount of value on your prowess on either the football field or cricket pitch. A high level of proficiency there tended to manifest as currency within the school community as a whole. As someone slight of build with poor eyesight and a level of co-ordination that definitely lacked any degree of sophistication, the First XI or First XVIII teams were never going to be the place for me. Cross country running it was for this future potential Harry Potter stunt double. Put one foot in front of the other, repeat, don't fall over. Oh and no requirement to be selected for a team – it's just you doing your thing. This approach to exercise and adventure would end up being a defining hallmark of almost every future endeavour that lay before me – albeit unbeknownst to me at the time.

After years of debating team and theatre performances the path forward was clear – get great marks, go to university, get a medical degree and become a doctor. I went to the Faculty of Medicine open day at Monash University and the dean addressed the thirty or so of us in the room.

'Out of the thirty of you here, 27 of you will fail to even get into this course.'

A quick scan of the room and I thought I identified two other people that looked reasonably intelligent and was then convinced that that made the three of us who would make it – tough luck for the remaining 27 that we would clearly leave behind in our soon to be medically qualified wake.

Fast forward to the end of the school year and I came up short. You needed a final score across all subjects of 95% to get into the fabled Monash medical degree. I got 93%. It would be the first of several huge jolting right hand turns in my life that would send my train on a vastly different route. I had a secondary choice of physiotherapy and a third choice of pharmacy. I got my third choice – no sprawling Monash University campus for me, instead it would be the relatively tiny satellite offshoot tucked away in inner city Melbourne - the Victorian College of Pharmacy.

Insert montage of university life, a sliding continuum where the study enthusiasm starts fairly high but slowly drifts down the scale as the freedom of an unfettered social life, inner city pub scene and the lure of the fine feminine form all collude to lead a young man to distraction. Life is to be lived of course. Four years of varying levels of commitment to study, a year of full-time work as an apprentice and suddenly I was entrusted with the dispensation of potions and pills for everything from scurvy to schizophrenia. I was working in the affluent seaside suburb of Mentone, ironically only a few hundred meters from my alma mater – but the station master was once again about to throw the switch on the tracks and send my life off on a turn that would see me leave Melbourne, never to return.

GO WEST YOUNG MAN

My boss had, seemingly very innocently, suggested I come in on my day off to meet a few pharmacists from regional Victoria who were in town doing a tour of pharmacies considered to be at the frontline of innovation in professional practice and customer care. I thought sure, why not. The story of what happened next and how the next decade of my life looked could fill an entire book on its own – but here's the cliff notes version.

The three pharmacists who had come to visit were salt of the earth kind of people – straight forward, unassuming and genuine. They had started a small, regional pharmacy group called HealthWise and were on what could be loosely described as a study tour. They were also recruiting, looking for future managers and pharmacy owners – and I fit the bill perfectly. I'm sure that the meeting was not by chance and that my boss knew that this would be an opportunity too great to miss for someone in my position, even though he would lose my services as a result. His unselfish foresight set me up for a decade of highs and lows, which ultimately would be the foundation for all my endeavours to come.

After a three-day tour across Western Victoria, I found myself packing my bags and moving from Melbourne, population roughly 4 million, to the town of Ararat, population roughly 7000. One main street, two pharmacies, one supermarket and, as I quickly found out, everyone knew everyone. I would spend two years there managing the pharmacy, living in a small two-bedroom flat along with the summer co-habitants of an endless stream of huntsmen spiders. If you've never seen one, google them. (I'll wait.) Over the summer months I simply couldn't sleep or shower without several of them taking up residence on the ceiling above me, or alongside me in the shower. Happy days.

From there a year spent further up the Western Highway in the slightly larger township of Horsham before my big break came to purchase a small pharmacy in the seaside regional hub of Warrnambool, population approximately 30,000. I arrived in April 2000, taking over a small pharmacy in the main street. The retiring owner told me I would either be here for one year or the rest of my life. I knowingly assured him it would only be the year.

I was a much better businessman than pharmacist and was here simply to turn the business around, install someone to manage it and move on. Two decades later, I'm living on the outskirts of Warrnambool on five acres of land along with my wife, two young boys, two dogs, eleven chickens, four cows and roughly two million (estimated) uninvited rogue rabbits. Those damn rabbits. Anyway, we've skipped ahead.

By the end of the year (2000) I would own three pharmacies, all within a few blocks of each other, and find myself working seven days a week, dedicating almost every waking hour to seeing how far I could take these businesses. The departing owner of the largest one – a behemoth of a business operating seven days a week from a beautiful heritage-listed, two-storey, corner building – scoffed at the sight of a 25 year old taking it all on, remarking that he doubted I would last a year. That was a red rag to a bull if there ever was one. I worked the next 365 days straight. A year later I had amalgamated the three businesses into two, purchased the freehold of the main one (in partnership with my parents) and promptly collapsed with exhaustion. Literally. A few days in hospital (ensconced in the kids ward no less, because they were full, not due to my diminutive stature I assure you) and the diagnosis was – slow down.

The next few years saw me do nothing of the sort. A dearth of pharmacists lead me to working longer and longer hours, neglecting my health and anything that even resembled good nutrition. I oversaw a huge expansion and renovation of my main pharmacy, in doing so making a friendship that has lasted a lifetime – one of the contractors, Zane, would go on to be one of my closest friends, our families still getting together every year even now, over two decades later.

But success is not without cost – and while I made every choice that placed me in the position I found myself in – there finally came a moment of clarity, it became evident that my health was, shall we say, sub-optimal, my consumption of fast food well beyond what would be considered a therapeutic dose and the stress was taking a toll on every aspect of my life. I was distant from family, in every sense. I had very few active friendships outside of my work circle and my partner of ten years and I had parted ways. The competing ties of work, distance and separation leaving both her and I with the realisation that it simply wasn't meant to be.

As a remedy for all of this I sought to break the glass and pull the fire alarm. I decided to do that by taking a holiday and going somewhere completely off of the beaten track, devoid of email, fax, wi-fi. Somewhere well off reservation for me, in an attempt to magically rebalance the books in one fell swoop.

And that's how I found myself flying into Tribhuvan Airport, Kathmandu, Nepal.

NAMASTE

By this time I had done some travelling, but all well and truly within the 'civilised first world'. A lack of pharmacists at home had seen me travel to the UK to recruit and my girlfriend at the time and I had managed to spend some time backpacking across Europe before my career well and truly took hold.

To this day I still remember vividly the car ride from the airport into central Kathmandu. The culture shock was short but sharp.

The sight of people living in shanties on the side of the road, burning rubbish in the dirt, feral dogs roaming the outskirts. The dust, the noise, the smells. But the shock was short lived, within moments it was replaced with a sense of wonder. This was exactly what I had been hoping for. Worlds apart from my current existence. I dropped my bags at the hotel and in what would become a hallmark standard operating procedure for me while travelling, bounced straight back out of the front door to walk the streets and see exactly what I had deposited myself into.

Time and distance have shrouded some of the memories of that trip but several are still prominent to this day – sitting on the banks of the Ganges watching families cremate their lost loved ones, walking the streets of Kathmandu under the ubiquitous fluttering prayer flags and colourful stupas.

I joined a small trekking crew and we flew to Lukla and headed into the Khumbu, all the way to Tengboche Monastery, nestled amongst the hills at 3860m above sea level. The previous township of Namche at approximately 3000 metres had already delivered a quick lesson in the power of gaining altitude, requiring me to spend an additional day there to juggle the twin demons of gaining altitude for the first time in my life and the impact of a culinary landscape that my gastro-intestinal system was also acclimatising to.

A cold morning at Tengboche and a self-imposed pre-dawn rise had me outside watching the sun rise over the Khumbu valley, Everest and Lhotse coming to life as the light struck their peaks and made its way down their respective faces to illuminate and begin warming the long valley below. I sat on the ground, among the quietly moving monks of Tengboche, surrounded by the tranquillity of prayer wheels, inhaling crisp, rarefied mountain air. I did not recognise it at the time but that moment, which I can still recall clearly to this day, represented the beginning of a seismic shift in my understanding of my place and significance in the world. I may be ultimately insignificant in an almost incomprehensibly large room – but on the flip side – what a playground. How could you not want to see what lay beyond the next rise?

That cold morning start in a tiny Sherpa village, home to a century old Tibetan Buddhist monastery and one-time home to Tenzing Norgay, marked the very beginnings of a long journey that is still unfolding.

GAINING ALTITUDE

I came home and jumped back into work but something had changed. There was a part of me that was now dedicated to going back and taking another step into that seemingly mystical world of snow and ice and adventure – a world that was vastly removed from my day-to-day reality.

I got back into running and suddenly my lunch breaks were no longer spent multi-tasking work and fast food, instead I'd dash home to hit the treadmill and grab a shower before rushing back to work. Over the next two years, two more adventures would fuel the fires within.

I headed north to Papua New Guinea to retrace the wartime footsteps of my maternal grandfather in Rabaul, New Britain. While there I trekked the famed Kokoda Track – a 96km dense jungle track in the rainforests of New Guinea, made famous by the exploits of the both the Australians and Japanese during World War II along with the local indigenous people, affectionately referred to as the 'fuzzie-wuzzies' by the Aussies on account of their distinct 'fuzzy' natural hairstyle.

Then there was my return to Nepal and the mountains, this time to scale Mera Peak. At 6,476m Mera is no small feat, but it doesn't present the technical challenges of complex climbing. It is considered one of the highest 'trekking' peaks – it's big but ultimately non-technical. Some basic mountaineering equipment and a stout body and mind will see you to the top without needing to invoke your 'inner Sherpa' to summit. An 18-day trip, with most of it on the move carrying packs and sleeping in tents, this was my first serious foray into a more alpine style trip. My first experience with an ice axe, crampons and being on a rope team – albeit a very basic one, perhaps almost unnecessary. It would be several years before I would return to this altitude (and higher) but the die was cast – I had stood on a summit, held my ice axe aloft and taken my 'summit selfie'. Deep within, a quiet but fierce evolution was taking place – something new was channelling its inner Yeats and sounding its 'barbaric yawp from the rooftop of the world'. This was an existence that I had never dreamed off – yet was captivated by. It was exhilarating – not just that moment on the summit but the entire process. The summit was 'simply' the culmination, the final project deliverable that belied the long train of work, both physical and mental, that had been laid down in preparation. Once again I didn't recognise it at the time, but somewhere a part of me was recognising the transformative power of the entire process of an endeavour such as this. From dream, to planning, to training, to execution. It would be years before I would come across this quote by motivational speaker Les Brown, but it was true long before I stumbled across it:

> 'When you are in pursuit of a dream, a transition takes place. And the transition is, what you become in the pursuit of the dream.'
> *Les Brown*

I had laid the foundation stones upon which I would soon build the next iteration of my life.

EXIT STAGE LEFT

The next couple of years back in the world of retail pharmacy would see two major events that would eventually send me spinning off into the depths of Antarctica. Literally.

The businesses continued to grow and eventually my ambition to take on every opportunity and the relentless pursuit of growth took its toll. I reached a point where I was working incomprehensible hours just to keep meeting supply deadlines and balance the vast number of projects I had simultaneously thrown into the air. I still remember crawling into bed one night to grab a meagre few hours before returning to work and feeling like someone had placed an anvil on my chest. I wasn't sure if I was about to have a heart attack or panic attack. Either way the message had been delivered. This is not going to end well. He who dies with the most money still dies. No medal, no sequel. I had to get out. I knew the journey out of the industry, specifically selling my business and untangling myself from HealthWise pharmacy group, which had now spread across two states, would be complex and time consuming. But the time had come – it was get out or die here. Your call.

The process of extricating myself from the businesses took the best part of eight months and was generally done in secret. Only my personal assistant, general manager and retail manager knew something was afoot. I wasn't in some mad hurry to exit but once the decision had been made there was no turning back. I knew it was the right decision and was keen to take a break and then see what life after 'retail' would look like.

The sale of the business was concluded in the middle of 2007. I had committed to stay on and work for a further three months to ensure a smooth transition – and after that I was free.

The end of 2007 and the early part of 2008 would see me generally living out of an orange Mountain Hardware tent in the middle of literally nowhere on one of three continents. In a summary that does no justice to the adventures themselves – over those few months I would travel to South America and then Antarctica to climb the Vinson Massif, home for a few weeks and then across to Tanzania to climb Kilimanjaro and finally back to South America to climb Aconcagua, the highest peak outside of the Himalayas standing just shy of 7000m above sea level. It was also somewhat of a trial by fire for my new-found relationship. My girlfriend at the time – who is now my wife and the mother of our two beautiful and adventurous boys – found herself newly entangled with a partner whose life, while exciting, involved a great degree of being ensconced on a far-flung mountainside, out of contact, more often than not.

Suffice to say adventuring and mountaineering had become well and truly entrenched. Over the next five years I would travel back to South America for a second season on Aconcagua, spend time in New Zealand refining technique and developing rescue and climbing skills before two years of trips to Denali in Alaska, culminating in a summit of Denali that would not only be my toughest but also ultimately put my climbing career on hold, sending me back in the direction of running – a journey that would go from the sublime to the ridiculous.

THE HIGH ONE

While my two expeditions on Denali could probably fill multiple chapters on their own, the journeys themselves were instrumental enough in my future career and adventuring direction that I feel some coverage is crucial – even if it is markedly abbreviated.

Denali is a monster. At 6190m above sea level, she is the highest peak on the North American continent. Beyond that it is a climb that demands the utmost respect of all who attempt it. While it doesn't have the final altitude of Everest, what it does have is a combination of natural and logistical challenges that work together to grind climbers down and send them home packing. The two years I was there, the summit success rate was just over 50%. To put that in perspective the summit success rate for Everest, according to the Himalayan Database, is closer to 65%.

The weather can be severe and unpredictable – to the point where there are three different weather reports each day for different altitudes on the mountain, and even then, they are simply a rough guide. Denali has a tendency to generate its own local weather patterns, in complete defiance of anything that may be happening in the surrounding area. Logistically there is just you – a short flight from the fly-speck town of Talkeetna and you are deposited at base camp (2200m above sea level) at the top of the wonderfully named Heartbreak Hill. There is no Sherpa or porter support, you carry your own gear plus your share of the group gear – this translates to each person having to carry around 60kg of equipment. When you only weigh around 70kg yourself, that makes for some heavy hauling. Thankfully, lower down you can spread the load between a backpack and a sled you will drag – but eventually the sheer incline makes sled usage impossible and it is slow, siege-style progression as we ferry loads uphill.

My first attempt at Denali would be a failed one. Coming into ABC (Advanced Base Camp) at 4300m I knew something was wrong. By this stage I had a very good understanding of how my body performed in these kind of environments and I knew something was amiss. I felt sluggish, was not holding anywhere near the pace I was capable of and was getting migraine type symptoms, despite never having suffered from them previously. At ABC the lead guide pulled me aside and gave me what I refer to as the 'hard chat'. She reminded me that from here it was a tough climb up a huge headwall before heading on to high camp – a place affectionately referred to as 'hell on earth'. And from there it was time for a summit attempt – a single day push that could last up to 20 hours depending on weather and performance. As all travel was done in rope teams this wasn't a case of, if you choose to turn back you can just head back down on your own. If you need to return we have to turn the entire rope team around and everyone's trip is over. We all go or we all fail. So either you can make it or you can turn around here at ABC and join a team that has already finished and is heading back down. Your call.

I slept on it and made the decision to turn tail and head back down – I knew something wasn't right and wasn't prepared to stack the summit success of my entire rope team on hope. Turns out it was the right call – a few days later back in Anchorage and I was stuck in my hotel room with a raging chest infection, barely able to get a full breath at sea level while doing nothing at all let alone while at altitude and working like a full-laden pack horse.

Once home again in Australia, I immediately committed to returning to Denali next climbing season, which meant I was a full year away from my return trip. Sure enough a year later I made the long return trip from Australia to Anchorage, Alaska, then onto Talkeetna and finally the short flight in a twin Otter to be once again delivered onto the Kahiltna Glacier and Denali base camp. This summit attempt would be a vastly different experience – I was stronger, fitter and better prepared mentally for the rigours of the journey having experienced much of the climb once already. Nineteen days after setting out from base camp we stood on the summit. Denali and the surrounding mountains would take their toll however that year – with six fatalities and 36 helicopter evacuations for the season. Denali National Park would be deadlier than Everest that year.

Our descent from the summit took just on two days, a far cry from the 19 day haul upwards. Lack of remaining supplies and a burning desire to get back to civilisation, a shower and real food is a great motivator. Finally landing back off the glacier into Talkeetna and I was utterly exhausted. I'm fairly certain that the enormous sugar-laden apple and cinnamon scroll, a pre-arranged treat awaiting us at the hangars, was the only thing keeping me on my feet.

This felt a far truer mountaineering expedition than all I had done before, I'd been stretched to my limits and had seen first-hand the cruel destruction that a mountain such as Denali can meter out – from the simple heart break of crushed summit dreams to the brutal reality of watching helicopters long-line bodies off the mountain.

As a single man, there is a certain risk versus reward profile that you are prepared to accept. It's a little easier to push the envelope with you're playing with no one's chips but your own. By the time I was coming off Denali with a successful but tough summit in the bag my situation had evolved. My ridiculously supportive girlfriend was now my wife and there was hopes for the expansion of our family in the coming years. Being frozen on a mountainside serves no purpose here. Further expeditions would have to be weighed against a different set of metrics. It felt right that it was time to hang the high-altitude boots up. Maybe not for good, but for now. They could take a well-earned rest after covering peaks in Africa, South and North America, Antarctica, New Zealand and the Himalayas.

As Henry Rollins says, we define ourselves through reinvention. It was time to take the fork in the road and see where it leads – it may lead me back full circle, or into an entirely different land.

Either way the direction and time was right.

The boots, harness and ice axe got packed and stored, I had married the woman I love and together we went from a team of two to a team of three and then finally four. But in among all of that there was still that identity of me. I had added the working titles of husband and father to my growing list of roles and responsibilities but I was still me – that release of the wilderness and the challenge of seeing what I was capable of still lurked in the background.

So I went back to what I knew – running. And once again the familiar path took shape. A short run lead to a longer one, then a half marathon, a full marathon – first on the road and then on the trails. Then a 50km race and then a two-day 80km trail race, individual and team events. I was back in the wilds and getting dirty, but without the inherent risk of scary acronyms like HAPE (high altitude pulmonary oedema) or HACE (high altitude cerebral oedema), hidden crevasses or slope-sweeping avalanches. I wasn't disappearing for months or more to climb and climb and climb.

A few years down that fork in the road and now I found myself with a fairly unique set of skills – I could run, for long distances, I was skilled and accustomed to operating in extreme cold, self-reliant and self-sufficient. I had placed my feet upon all seven continents and there were only a few places on the planet that I still wanted to make my mark upon. Ironically, sitting in my office at home, surfing the internet would open the door to a journey of over 14,000km to the one of the most remote places on Earth.

lessons

LESSON 1

The stories we tell ourselves

IT'S RELENTLESS. ALL DAY, EVERY DAY. At times carefully structured and curated, other times freewheeling and careening about, bounding from edge to edge. It's the internal dialogue, the endless narrative continuously reviewed, rebuilt and replayed in our minds, constantly echoed by your very own in-house, impossible to evict, and potentially somewhat crazy roommate. That very same voice upstairs that is reciting this book, in your head, this very instant. That roommate is crafting 'your story' – and given that we are the story we tell ourselves then surely we want the best damn story we can produce. No one wants to direct a flop or some insipid tale populated with bland featureless characters and a story arc that meanders without colour or shape. We want the blockbuster – whether it's a Spielberg adventure epic, a rollicking tale of excitement and twists and turns, or a thought-provoking mystery of interlacing identities and nuanced layers of understanding. Either way we want the award-winning story of all stories – our story.

The greatest ones have it all – conflict, struggle, drama, emotions, adventure, excitement, loss, discovery – all those components that bring stark, bright light and contrasting shade to our lives. They are complex, layered, convoluted and often lack clarity at the time but become clearer with development and reflection. Like any great tale, yours will require editing, refinement, crafting, cajoling and plenty of purposeful direction. Few will spend a life of free-wheeling carelessness and be left standing with anything other than a collection of seemingly disparate scenes. Like a masterful director you will need to not only craft incredible individual scenes but also find a way to weave those parts into a broader narrative of the whole – the unique identity that is you. See and celebrate the little breadcrumbs along the way while simultaneously melding them towards a greater opus.

The quality and substance of this directorial debut boils down to two distinct questions– what am I capable of, and what am I worth? In my life that has manifested as the 'quest for adventure' and the 'question of value'.

ADVENTURES – WHY YOU NEED THEM AND HOW TO HAVE THEM

I once spent a month trekking and climbing in the Andes, carrying a long PVC pipe, which was full of my own poo.

I was on an expedition to climb the highest peak on the South American continent and the highest peak anywhere outside of the Himalayas. Part of the process is to obtain a climbing permit from local park rangers and one of the conditions of that permit is that you will leave no waste behind. And I mean no waste. Hence the tube – they issue you with a permit and a pipe. On your return to the rangers station you relinquish your pipe and it is weighed. Based on how long you were climbing for they compare the weight against a standardised table – if it is within the range for the time away you are free to go. Underweight and you are fined as it is assumed that you 'left something behind' and if it is overweight the office staff give you a resounding round of applause for over-achieving. True story (I may have embellished the standing ovation but you get the point).

Over the last two decades I have been fortunate enough to find myself in some very strange places on the planet doing some rather extreme things. The poo story, to be honest, is just the tip of the iceberg – we haven't even talked (yet) about the time I drank a shot of whiskey with a preserved human toe in it, in a bar, in a frontier town in the Yukon. Or the time I made a 'voluntary' donation to the Maoist Party in the depths of the Himalayas so I could continue on my way 'unhindered'. And then there was the Russians, but we will get to that.

Bottom line – adventures, those seemingly wild expeditions outside the careful laid bounds of your 'normal life' – provide the very best 'bang for buck' when it comes to taking the story that is you up a notch. It's that very moment that we test the mettle, extend ourselves and attempt something that seems beyond reach, scope or reason, that we give our story the opportunity to develop a chapter full of revelation, growth and excitement – regardless of the outcome. The best stories are often framed against backdrops of failures, hardship and tough love.

I guarantee that yours will be no exception. So if adventures are the express lane to building a tale worth telling, why aren't we all running off in the wild blue yonder? Turns out there are a few common roadblocks – so to help you charge forth and have your own adventure, let's have a look at what they are and how to knock them out of the way.

ROADBLOCK 1 – THE CRISIS OF FAITH

We've all had it – if not once then multiple times. Some call it the crisis of faith, or the imposter syndrome, a sudden and vast retreating of the tide that was my self-confidence before it vanished towards the horizon and left me stranded on the shore. In my speedos. Alone. Wondering what the hell am I doing here?

I've had those moments multiple times in my life, but keeping with the adventure theme, let's pick a suitably Indiana Jones-style one. It was December 2009 and I was boarding a retro-fitted Russian Ilyushin Il-76 military cargo plane. The Ilyushins were quintessentially Russian, utilitarian, spartan, rugged and designed to work unwaveringly in the harsh Soviet and Siberian winters. I was boarding it in the fly-speck town of Punta Arenas at the very southern tip of South America. We were about to embark on the six-hour flight that would deposit us at a place called Patriot Hills, deep in Antarctica. I looked around as I nervously fiddled with the webbing on the side of the plane – no finding Seat 12C and stowing your bags overhead here.

The entire centre of the plane was crammed with sleds of supplies destined for the many expeditions and research stations on the white continent. Rows and rows of fuel drums and equipment. My fellow adventurers, explorers, guides and researchers squeezed along the side of the plane, finding a spot on the hard bench seats that ran the length of the plane and strapping in. *What in the actual hell am I doing here?* I'm a pharmacist from a rural town in Australia, bespectacled and slight of frame. Far more Potter than Shackleton. Yet beside me were an array of men and women who looked no more concerned than if they were boarding the 7am flight from Melbourne to Sydney. But they all had that air, that poise, of people who despite the smiles and relaxed manner, possessed a hardness of character that most likely had been carved from stone. Obdurate stone at that. They just looked hard as nails. I felt soft as butter in comparison. *Repeat: what the hell am I doing here?*

Over the next three weeks I would live in a tent in -40c, drag a loaded sled day in and day out and endure never-ending sunlight to finally stand on the summit on the highest point at the bottom of the Earth, the Vinson Massif, Ellsworth Ranges, Antarctica.

'Two paths diverged in the woods and I —
took the one less travelled by.
And that has made all the difference...'
Robert Frost

The crisis of faith occurs not because we are unworthy but because we are not ready to believe in ourselves – our worth, our ability, our capacity to do far more than we credit ourselves with.

Because we have forgotten that such a crisis is normal – it's part of the process. Being scared, nervous, unsure, even failing – doesn't make you weird or less or wrong – it makes you human. It makesyou normal. The sooner you can make peace with the knowledge that failure (potential or otherwise) is simply a regular part of the process and not some cosmic signal that you're not welcome or not meant to be writing this particular chapter of your story, the easier it all becomes. It's just part of the development of your story, embrace it.

For me that crisis occurred right in the thick of it, literally as the wheels left the tarmac – but perhaps your crisis begins far earlier, on the couch, in the office, awake at night. Wondering if you are made of the 'right stuff' to chase whatever adventure that's whispering away inside. Well, here's the good news – you are already fully qualified to have an epic adventure – because your mere existence makes you the most successful explorer, conqueror, warrior, poet and pioneer in the history of the world. Let me explain.

ROADBLOCK NO 2 – THE RIGHT STUFF

As you know, by the end of high school I was a fully-fledged nerd. Debate club, theatre club, Dungeons and Dragons, zero athletic ability. Like, none. My 'chosen' sport was cross country running – because you didn't have to get picked for a team and the athletic requirements were one foot in front of the other, don't fall over, repeat. I would go on to be a pharmacist and eat plenty of fast food and get really good at PlayStation.

Fast forward a few decades and I'm deep inside the Arctic circle, dragging a sled, -35c and howling winds. I'd drag that sled for just eight days, 24 hours a day, living on only a few 20-40 minute naps a day. This was the 6633 Arctic Ultra, a 614km self-supported, single stage race, one of the toughest races in the world. That's a pretty big disconnect from the Harry Potter body-double to full Bear Grylls mode. How did that happen?

Here's a hint – he was born for it.

Let's have a quick biology lesson and then a short history lesson.

Biology 101 – you are the physical expression of your DNA, the genetic code embedded in virtually every cell of your body. Stretched out the DNA in an individual cell would be around 3m in length, and at a low ball estimate you have around 10 trillion cells, give or take the few cells that you are busy shedding onto the seat, floor, the person next to you, right now. That DNA is the composite of your parents, 50/50.

But to give you that DNA your parents had to do something very special – no not just 'love each other in a very special way' as my sex-education teacher would put it, they had to survive. And not just them, but their parents and their parents and their parents and so on and so on. Think about it, start small scale and then zoom right out. In the last century alone your parents and grandparents and great grandparents had to survive two World Wars, survive disease, live without Facebook, avoid being hit by a bus or dying of a genetic abnormality before they had a chance to meet the love of their life and pass on their DNA. If their DNA tripped on any of those hurdles your DNA died with them. If they died childless on Flanders Fields, on the beaches of Gallipoli – your DNA died with them. Your ancestors survived, through luck or skill or divine intervention, but they are survivors.

Go back further, your DNA survived the Black Plague, it never died on a battlefield clutching sword and shield, it was never savaged beyond repair by a marauding Viking, a sabre tooth tiger or stampeding mammoth.

You come from a long line of winners. Of survivors, of the strong, the adventurous, the brave. You are already made of 'the right stuff'. Your DNA crossed the seas in search of new lands. It fought the marauding hordes, never got fatally struck by lightning or was the unfortunate recipient of a 'Darwin Award' (Darwin Awards are given to people who, through spectacular stupidity, graciously removed themselves from the gene-pool, saving us from future generations of equally poor decision-making. To give you an example one of the 2018 recipients died because he decided that upon spotting what he thought was an injured but fully grown bear the prudent course of action would be to stop, get out of the car and try to take a selfie with it. His friends in the car got out to film it, and in doing so provided spectacular if gruesome video footage of their friend's untimely demise at the claws of a very un-injured and recently disturbed fully grown bear). Trust me – you come from a very long line of winners. Science will have it no other way – for you to be here, right now, your DNA literally climbed out of the primordial slime and fought its way through victory after victory after victory to end up here.

You are, by default, the all-conquering genetic hero of a thousand, thousand battles. Still think you could never have an adventure? You are the current pinnacle of nature's endless job application.

In reality you probably feel somewhat less marauding and conquering Viking and more, office worker, parents and teachers committee member, personal Uber driver for your kids. So where did you put your axe and shield? What happened?

We began in tribes. You had a group, most likely family, and you had a role, an identity. Hunter, gatherer, warrior, parent, leader.

We expanded, explored, conquered, we were the savages, the barbarians, the wolves at the door. If you couldn't fulfil that role then you most likely got dropped from the team – not because the team didn't want you, but because nature demands it. Get gored by a sabre-tooth – sorry you're out. Can't find food or water – thanks for playing. Got a mild infection a few thousand years before antibiotics – please exit stage left.

Then came the great monotheistic religions, the continent-spanning empires, the dawn of modern politics and finally the all-pervasive corporations – such as the FAANG gang – Facebook, Amazon, Apple, Netflix and Google.

All of this – from Zarathustra to Zuckerberg – has strived to achieve the same goal. The dilution of individual identity. Your individual identity. The unique and great individual story that is you.

The great religions – you can worship who or what you want as long as the overarching deity is the one we tell you. And over time we whittle away until your festivals are our festivals and the old Gods have been replaced with the new.

'Civis Romanus' – I am a citizen of Rome, you can retain your village or tribal identity as long as you recognise the overarching power of the Roman Empire, or the British Empire, the Western Empire, our Empire.

Boomer, Gen X, Millennial – are you Labor or Liberal, monarchist or republican, Mac or Windows? Welcome to the largest generic tribes humanity has ever known.

Ask anyone who has ever managed a business with a sizeable inventory, ask anyone in a warehouse, which is easier – stocking a million of the same part or stocking a million individually unique parts? Interchangeable is manageable, they are controllable and fundamentally – easily replaceable.

You were once a fearsome hunter, a brave explorer, a warrior poet, maybe even a conqueror. Generations passed and we became villagers, farmers, factory workers, and now finally we have evolved into mere data, metadata, a trackable, predictable, readily manipulated, moveable wallet.

I believe that deep down on some level we are aware of this slow but determined erasure of uniqueness and identity. The endless assault on the self. Sadly, a small number of those in power will use this knowledge, the smell of that undercurrent of resentment, of feeling lost at sea, to rally us back into the tribes that they want, tribes with no purpose other than to vilify the 'other tribe'. To galvanise that rising tide of unconscious need for identity and belonging to further their own causes and agendas. Us versus them.

This is why you must fight to find yourself, to define yourself not by the yardsticks of others, not by the value that society places upon you, but by the measures and meanings that you value yourself. On your own terms. Terms that give colour and shape and meaning and depth to your life. So when they ask, 'what happened?', you will have a story to tell. Your story.

ROADBLOCK NO 3. BUT I'M NOT AN ATHLETE

How the hell am I meant to go have some epic adventure?
I'm a parent, I've got commitments, I'm out of shape, I'm scared.
I'm not some elite athlete.
News flash.
Neither am I.
I'm just a nerdy Dad.
With commitments.
Who used to be out of shape.
And who still gets scared.

I've hiked the famed Kokoda Track in the jungles of Papua New Guinea twice. You can tackle the Kokoda Track in one of two ways – with a porter (a local who carries the bulk of your supplies and equipment) or without. The first time I trekked the Track I did so with a porter. I turned up in my latest hiking boots and moisture wicking top, ready for 96km of mountainous jungle trails. My porter turned up in shorts and flip-flops. I don't think he broke a sweat. I most certainly did - before we even started. I returned almost a decade later – older and far more experienced. No porter, stronger, fitter, wiser – and had an entirely different experience. Think of my first attempt as 'work in progress', and the second as a finished product.

There is a disconnect for people when they read my bio, then meet me in person. They read the list of mountains. races and adventures and expect some kind of Bear Grylls/Chuck Norris character to appear – then I turn up, looking much more Daniel Radcliffe's body double fresh off the Harry Potter set. Less with the Chuck Norris, more with the boy-wizard.

It's my hope that that disconnect immediately opens a mental door for people – to not look at the list of things I've done but to realise that I look a lot like them. I'm not an Olympian, I'm not an astronaut, I haven't had to overcome some epic personal tragedy - I'm just normal. It provides an opportunity to immediately bury the excuse of 'well I couldn't do anything like what he has done because he's special/unique/talented/gifted'. What you are left with is, 'He looks and sounds a lot like me, how did he do all that stuff?'.

That opens a huge doorway – an opportunity to take the first step 'outside' and maybe, just maybe, start to think about what you, as a 'normal' person might be capable of. That's where I come in, to start to highlight the doors, the possibilities. To remind them that failure is just a part of the process.

As I've mentioned, Denali ('The High One' in Athabascan) is one tough climb. My first attempt was cut short by something as simple as a decent bout of the flu. A year of training, months of planning and sacrifice, flying half-way around the world, all thrown out one day before summit day thanks to a virus I probably picked up at the airport. Went home, recovered and started again. And a year later, almost to the day, stood on the summit of the highest point on the North American continent.

I have accrued my fair share of 'DNF' (did not finish) in my time – both on big mountains and in races. In some cases I've turned back at the very last hurdle – mere hours from a summit after weeks of climbing, in some cases I've pulled the plug on big ultra races barely having made the half-way mark. But in every case I learnt a great deal, earned my scars and as Kipling put it, stooped down with worn out tools and started again. And in every case, I have gone back, wiser, battle-hardened and better prepared and – in every case – got the job done.

So why don't I consider myself an athlete? Well if you went through high school with me you'd already know the first reason, and probably be laughing at the concept of me as an 'athlete', remember – more boy wizard, less Hulk.

To me real 'athletes' do have the capacity to be truly the best of the best in an already elite field, the 0.1%. They often do have some measure of a genetic head start and have then leveraged that through hard graft, the relentless hours of training, sacrifice and dedication.

Ok Mr 'Non-Athlete' – that still sounds a lot like you, you've climbed it, trekked it, raced it, even won it.

True, but I've achieved those milestones and climbed those mountains not through being athletically gifted – I've done it through hard graft, discipline and the knowledge that as a regular person I may not have your VO2 max, or supercharged mitochondria, but I will out-work you and I will remain mentally and emotionally steadfast despite all that the mountains and races can throw at me – and that is not a unique skillset. **Not a boon of genetics.**

To some degree I believe that the fact that I don't label myself as an athlete has been liberating – I have no expectations of what I should or shouldn't be able to achieve – all I can do is go out and see what I'm capable of. No one expects the nerdy Dad to win. Find that limit, whatever it is, place a stake in the ground and then see if we can move it a little further tomorrow. And do that over and over and over.

That's the discipline.

That's the mindset.

That's the sacrifice.

None of these skills require being genetically blessed or gifted. They require you to be a proactive and self-aware human being, and to do the work. Learn (test and measure), work hard and be willing to push the envelope – especially when it comes to being mentally and emotionally uncomfortable. If that sounds like it might be hard – it is. It also requires no special equipment or memberships or literally anything. Money, access, connections – none of these things are limiting factors. It is all up to you and if you are willing to do the work then there is literally nothing halting you.

The last argument is – 'yes that's all well and good but I'm not you. Mental fortitude and all that resilience stuff I couldn't do that – I'm just an accountant, office dweller, home body, mum, Dad, plumber, lawyer, insert label'. We saddle ourselves with a shiny label and then yield to its weight. We let it define us, use it to determine what we are capable of, what we should or shouldn't be doing. Worst of all, we let it tell us what we are worth.

How we value ourselves.

How we define ourselves.

How we let society value us.

This has enormous implications that we are often too busy, too tired or too blinded to see.

It's time to talk about the elephant in the room.

You are not your job.

LESSON 1 - SUMMARY

1. Look for Adventure – We build our identity out of the stories that make up our lives, and great stories run the full gamut of human experience – love, loss, drama, passion, fear, excitement, struggle, conquest. Don't shy away from adventure because of the risk, instead use them as a gateway to access all those magnificent puzzle pieces that create your mosaic.

2. Dodge the Roadblocks
    a. The crisis of faith – take the path less travelled and believe in yourself. Being scared, unsure, even failing – simply makes you normal. So be at peace with all of these emotions and outcomes and go forth anyway.

    b. The Rght Stuff – remember your primordial spark of existence. You are the tip of countless generations of survivors, adapters, adventurers and explorers – so start acting like it.

    c. Drop the Labels – athlete, adventurer, entrepreneur – these are all just labels that you can choose to be burdened by or simply jettison. Learn to value and define yourself on your own terms.

LESSON 2

You are not your job.

'SO PAUL, WHAT DO YOU DO?'

'Take a seat mate, this will take a while...'

Give a different answer, get a different response. Tell them I'm a pharmacist (which is true) and you can see the mental cogs turning, making a host of conscious/unconscious assumptions on income, education, likely political affiliation. Tell the next person I'm a personal trainer (which is true) and we get a fresh suite of assumptions. Tell them I drive a forklift in a warehouse (which was true, I also have an MBA and built the company) and the cogs turn again. But the underlying premises are the same, you have a blue/white collar job, degree/no degree, this income, that income, ipso facto you are worth 'this'.

It gets really interesting when I answer with, 'I'm a stay-at-home Dad'. That tends to grind the cogs to a halt. Generally, I get a raised eyebrow and an 'oh...' You can see that they're doing the mental arithmetic but keep getting stuck. *Can he not work? What's his wife do? Yeah but what else do you do?* The mental friction comes from the way we define and therefore value ourselves – especially as men. Without knowing 'what I do' in terms of a paying job, people are suddenly left with no frame of reference for valuing me, my worth, my contribution or my standing among others, especially other men. Suddenly I'm some kind of enigma.

For a long stretch the nature of the workforce helped dictate and reinforce what were long considered standard gender roles – Dad worked and provided financially and Mum ran the household and shouldered the vast daily burden of raising the progeny. The nature of work, especially through the twentieth century, helped cement that. Industrialisation, manufacturing, primary industry, war – all these fostered an advantage to those better suited to physical labour. Literally, the strong were favoured. In the US census of 1970, a census that covered almost two-hundred million humans, the number of men who listed there occupation as 'stay-at-home Dad' was…six. That's not a typo, it was six out of roughly one-hundred million men.

Then the workforce dynamics changed as the industrial revolution gave way to a cerebral and then digital one, the workforce ideal moved from a preference for brawn to brain – from hardware to software. As manufacturing jobs moved or vanished and the information age, mobility of work and automation gained greater ascension, men found the ground shifting under their feet and women found themselves no longer behind the strength curve. Unlike raw horsepower and load-carrying capacity, IQ is not gender biased.

Here's the rub – if you have valued your 'worth' based primarily on your capacity for financial provision and identify yourself as a title rather than a fully-fledged, multi-faceted human being, then when the goal posts moved (and in an evolutionary sense they moved incredibly fast) there was a sudden margin-call on your leveraged sense of self-worth.

As men particularly we have a strong tendency to define our own value based on our ability to 'provide'. If I am not the breadwinner then who am I? This is brought into stark relief when we move from being partners to parents. The arrival of a new 'diminutive overlord' triggers either the opportunity to redefine, or alternatively reinforces stereotypes and stigma.

Looking at the Australian example, in the 1991 census 33% of women identified themselves as stay-at-home mums (SAHM), only 4% of men classified themselves as stay-at-home dads (SAHD). Fast forward to 2016 (not even a generation) and the SAHM percentage has dropped by 6% and the SAHD percentage has increased…by 1%. Where did everyone go? They went back to work – the percentage of households with both parents working went from 52% to 61% for the same period. The drivers behind this are many and varied but I feel that two stand out (and one lurks in the background).

First, those changing workforce dynamics I discussed earlier gave women a greater opportunity to move back into the workforce in a manner and style that started to feel more like a level playing field. The second driver was financial. Everyone loves seeing the equity in their home escalate and their share portfolio climb the ladder, but too often we forget that that comes at a cost. Your home is only worth what the market will pay for it – so if the value is increasing that means that someone is paying, and then having to pay that off. The race to the top of the supposed 'financial success' mountain brought with it a simultaneous slide into the darker valleys of endless work. Single-income households with evenings and weekends free from pervasive email and non-social social media moved to the pressures of balancing double-income life with permanent connectivity to the office via digital intrusion. We built a temple and then promptly locked ourselves inside of it.

The final lurking background driver hides in that conundrum of 'parental leave'. Regardless of the moniker we attach to it – maternity leave, parental leave, primary carer leave, secondary carer leave – it shines a light on what we have come to value.

For men parental leave can bring with it a surreptitious undertone of 'loss'. What am I giving up? Don't get me wrong, as men the unbridled joy of being with your newborn, of that immediate sense of a new family is magical. But for many, lurking in the back of our minds, is that thought that while I am *here* I am not *there* – that innate modern societal drive that I should be/need to be breadwinning, not allowing the corporate deck chairs to rearrange themselves in my absence. The mortgage doesn't change, our household budget has just taken a radical left turn – there is that hidden sense of urgency to get back to the 'status quo'. In the face of crippling uncertainty about our ability to suddenly master new skills – everything from nappy changing to the not-so-subtle art of living with sleep deprivation – our workplace seems like a safe haven. There are rules, expectations, traditions – and co-workers tend to manage their own bowel movements rather than requiring your close-action support. More importantly I know who I am there, where I fit and – this is a big one – I know my value. And all financial arguments and pressures are real and pressing – but perhaps deeper into that valley, far from the light on the mountain top, is that nagging fear that if I'm not the breadwinner, if I have lost that responsibility, then what is my value? How do I derive my sense of self-worth? Where is my place in my tribe if I am no longer seated at the head of the table.

And finally all of this is coloured with two overtones – money and masculinity. Let's start with money. Tyler Durdin was right – you're not your job, or your khakis, or your furniture. But for many that metric of net financial capacity or position has become all consuming – primarily because we don't have an alternative metric that we are comfortable with. Or perhaps more importantly – a metric that everyone in our circle seems to be comfortable with. If I hand over the keys for financial provision and all the decision making associated with that title – what do I have left? Workforce dynamics used to make this decision easier to negotiate – 'he' who earns more should remain at work to provide financially. That argument has all but vanished as brainpower is favoured over brawn, so on a purely financial basis, often the best decision is that Dad does stay at home. That brings us to the second overtone – masculinity.

My goal here isn't to delve into the murky depths of 'toxic masculinity' or the (to me) inexplicable rise of the #dadbod. Not to say that these issues aren't real or require rigour – that's for another time and place. Side stepping the heat, emotion and hyperbole, just consider for a moment the traditional concept of masculinity and the reality of where many of us find ourselves now. From the scientific to the fictional, the classic male was the Freudian archetype – psychologically (and physically) strong, dominant, assertive, decisive and 'successful'. The alternative depictions in the realms of fiction saw us devolved simply to either the dad-bodded comic relief, the anti-jock or finally the broken and dangerous.

So what the hell do we do now?

We re-define ourselves.

Not in terms of our job. Not in terms of our earning capacity – but in terms of what we really, honestly, bring to the table. And that process can be scary as hell.

In my experience, developing (and considering) yourself to be multi-faceted serves not only as a great hedge against feeling like your value is lost due to one single seismic shift, but it also allows you to see how deep and far your abilities run.

More and more I find myself using the phrase, 'I'm the father of two young boys'. A strong component of my self-worth is increasingly derived from my capacity and part in raising them both as a SAHD. I often use the example that when I was in Year 12, I had my life planned out – I was going to get a medical degree, become a doctor and my business card would reflect as such. Decades later and my business card is devoid of the term 'doctor', but it carries a myriad of others – mountain climber, adventurer, entrepreneur, pharmacist, speaker, husband, father, son, brother, nerd. All those personas bring value and joy into my life – at varying times and in varying ways.

So take some time to reflect on who you are and what you do beyond the narrow definitions of your title at the office, or the role that society has deemed you fit to fill. Revel in your complexity – it is your shield against the storm and your banner in battle.

And there is no rule that says once you have come to some semblance of comfort with your identity and value that it's suddenly carved in stone. All manner of nature and nurture will contrive to shift the sands beneath your feet so that your role, and strengths and weaknesses, will rise and fall with the tides.

As a current addendum at the time of writing much of the world is under some form of lock down as we negotiate the labyrinth of a COVID-19 world. For many of us that has meant that work is either remote, on hold or just straight up cancelled. If you had identified as the household breadwinner out 'in the trenches' every day and may now suddenly find yourself in unfamiliar territory. Your 'office' looks a lot like home and your significant other may well be the 'alpha persona' running a tight ship — suddenly your role has drastically changed. If you don't carry with you a strong internal sense of the value you bring beyond your job then this may be some very confronting times indeed.

You are more than your job. You bring values beyond your resume — remember that. Embrace it. Find ways you can bring those values and skills and strengths to play in the new environment — it may mean some humble pie, some false starts, some discovery of 'gaps' in your resume for the 'new normal'. That's ok — it just makes you human. The key is to see this as evolution, you are not a finished product nor a static beast, cast in stone. You retain the right, at all times, to recast the bones, to push all your chips into the pot, to recast your future.

LESSON 2 - SUMMARY

Society loves to pigeonhole, to label, to allocate and define. It makes people feel more comfortable, putting everything in its assigned 'place'. It is also a trap, like being placed in a windowless, doorless room. You can choose to accept that room and live within its confines or decide to walk about the entire house.

Embrace change, challenge, be undefined and unconventional. Do not become trapped by the definition of you that exists on your business card or job title. Let it be a part of you – but a scene, not your entire story.

You are a never-ending work in progress – keep evolving.

LESSON 3
Go

SO STEP ONE – STOP GIVING A SHIT about the labels. Want to do something, have an adventure, run a race, start something new? Then do it. You don't have to be Sir Edmund Hillary or Shackleton, Steve Jobs or Chuck Norris – because you are already all of those things. Remember – you are literally stuffed to the brim with the DNA of generations of winners. So dig up that primordial spark and realise that you have everything you need.

You are a functioning, living, breathing, thinking human being. Therein lies every capacity and tool you will ever need. Sure a few of those things may require some 'dusting off', some tinkering around the edges. Perhaps a little less ice cream here and a little more self-belief there. A little more sleep and a little less Netflix, a little more fresh air and a little less Instagram.

What happens next – who knows? That's the beauty of 'choose your own adventure'. Start here and go forth. Maybe it's a fun run that leads to a marathon that leads to an ultra-marathon that leads to you tackling and winning the windiest, coldest and toughest ultramarathon in the world (or is that just me…). Or maybe it starts with finding those things that aren't work or a new TV or a cracker Instagram post, but are truly valuable to you and start telling yourself that story. I'm the father of two young boys. I'm also a pharmacist and a speaker and an entrepreneur and adventurer. But that statement, 'I'm a stay-at-home father of two young boys' and all that statement entails, fills my life with joy, colour, fulfilment, sleep deprivation and the all-pervasive smell of a nappy that is in immediate need of changing before we find ourselves elbow deep in a full scale bio-containment failure. Value yourself. Believe in yourself. Give yourself permission to try.

It won't be easy. There will be struggle, setbacks, failure, hardship. That's what makes it worthwhile. That's what brings about the change and growth and evolution.

It's all on you. So act. It's the practice of little but continual displays of self-belief, the small wins of getting the training done or changing that behaviour, of valuing what truly matters to you.

Choose an adventure.

Plant a flag and say I am starting from here and I am going there.

Remember you come from a long line of winners and conquerors and survivors and adventurers. Accept that there will be bumps in the road, twists, turns, maybe even the odd derailment. But have the mindset of continual, perpetual forward momentum. No matter how small, or how tough, keep moving forward. Inch by inch if need be. The key here is not to get buried by the day-to-day grind of some of those seemingly very small steps but to remember that these are all daily deposits into an account that is earning compounding interest. Every piece added will bear more than its fair share in contribution to the end goal. Keep moving forward. This is how you craft a mind and body that is ready to take on your next adventure.

So next time someone asks – 'what happened?' – you can tell them a true story - a chapter of your story. It may not be about spending a month carrying your own poo in a PVC pipe on a mountainside – in fact it will probably be better.

It will be an amazing story.

Because it will be your story.

LESSON 3 - SUMMARY

Have a mindset that is set to a default position of action. Do. Go. Act.

Remember that any forward momentum towards your goal is still forward momentum – and seen as part of the bigger picture all contribute to that ever-growing account of work, of effort, of development. Those actions all add up and build upon each other, often in ways we do not or cannot see at the time – even the failures.

Don't look for validation or motivation or discipline from outside. The most powerful form of discipline, the one that delivers the greatest gains – is self-discipline. So have the discipline to do what has to be done. Every time.

Choose an adventure and go build your story.

part two

THE TOUGHEST RACE
(FIRST ATTEMPT AT 6633 ARCTIC ULTRA)

CHAPTER 3

The 13 toughest races in the world

Warrnambool, Victoria, Australia.
April 2016

IT'S ALL *OUTSIDE MAGAZINE*'S FAULT.

Well, them and Facebook.

Here I was innocently scrolling through my Facebook feed when up pops an article from Outside Magazine entitled, '13 Toughest Races in the World'. This is essentially prime clickbait material for a semi-reformed alpinist with a bag of ultra marathons under their belt wondering what to do next. A minuscule mouse click and a couple of scrolls later and there it was – the 6633 Arctic Ultra. The description was the literary equivalent of the show window at your local patisserie – the epic show-stopper cake (in this case the image of a lone figure dragging a sled across a vast frozen Arctic expanse) stops you in your tracks, then your gaze works its way along the metaphorical shelves, the psychological restraints are unshackled one by one and before you know it you're inside, seated and doing your darnedest to send your blood glucose reading into the stratosphere.

'Competitors tackle the entire distance completely unsupported'
'Pushing almost 600km deep into the Arctic Circle'
'Katabatic winds, temperatures regularly into the -30C'
'Only 11 finishers in 7 years'

A millisecond of Google searching later and we are neck deep in race result spreadsheets, archived race reports, mandatory gear lists and the obligatory warnings about the seriousness of such an endeavour.

Boxes that it instantly ticked:

1. Arctic Circle – I had climbed or raced on all seven continents, but a true foray into the Arctic Circle had thus far eluded me. Here was a chance to tick off the top of the planet, giving me the 'full set'.

2. An ultra of ultras – the distance was both completely mind boggling and ridiculously alluring – 580km.

3. No altitude – the risk of not clipping onto a rope correctly while perched precariously on a narrow ice-encrusted rock ledge with a 3000m drop below you – all with a mind clouded by hypoxia – was not going to be a factor. It would be freezing, exhausting and epically challenging but the slew of risks that come with high altitude work would be non-existent.

4. Canada – the Yukon, Northwest Territories, home of frontiersmen, the Iditarod, the Klondike, the Dempster, the Mackenzie Delta. There was real palpable history here, the savage frozen north lit by the green plasma waves of the northern lights. This was home to adventures worthy of tale.

When it comes to assessing an event or expedition like this I have a mental framework, a guide I use to test whether this is something that I am truly committed to sacrifice time for – time to train, time away from family – as well as the sacrifices I am asking of others, especially family. Is this a flight of fancy or a true response to that savage within, itching to be let out and cast against the elements? The framework exists in the form of two internal hurdles.

The first hurdle – wait thirty days before I do or say anything. Just go about my everyday life and see how often the race pops into my head. If I get to the end of the thirty days and I haven't really thought about it that much then I'm not truly serious. If I've thought about it every day – dreamed, plotted, imagined, visualised – then this is something I am truly ready to commit to. The second hurdle is in the form of a question – if I could do this but I could never tell anyone about it, and no one would ever know I did it, would I still do it? In other words, am I doing this because I must, for me and me alone or am I doing it to be able to satisfy some validation from others? What is my true motivation – intrinsic or extrinsic?

Both hurdles were cleared for the 6633 without contest. After a month I had thought of nothing else, my spare mental capacity immediately re-purposed to planning, envisioning, questioning, daydreaming. This was not going to go away. The second hurdle was similarly cleared – no one had ever heard of this race, it's not like it was the UTMB (Ultra Trail Du Mont Blanc) attracting the very cream of endurance racing. It was virtually unknown, held in a part of the world so sparsely inhabited it may as well be the moon. I could do it and shout from the roof tops and still no one would know what I was talking about. This was for me.

So sure enough, a month after reading that Outside magazine

article, over breakfast one morning I casually asked my wife her thoughts on me going to Canada (an incredibly safe first world country as I immediately pointed out) to take part in an 'adventure race' (not a highly dangerous mountaineering expedition) for a measly few weeks – probably three weeks away door to door. She gave it the green light of approval – and unknown to both us, started a journey that would not only leave a deep and indelible imprint on the next three years of our lives, but also dramatically change both my outlook and trajectory for years far beyond.

It was time to train and prepare.
We had work to do.

CHAPTER 4
Rise & grind

Warrnambool, Victoria, Australia
2016–2017

ARE YOU GETTING THE ADAPTATION you want or are you just getting better at suffering?

The danger lies in the fact that you don't know what you don't know. My training plan for my 2017 attempt at the 6633 looked sound and considered – on paper – but I look back now with the wisdom of hindsight and the gaps are glaring. Ironically, it was those exact gaps and failings that allowed me to come back in 2019 an entirely different athlete – and person for that matter. The gaps in the foundations I laid in training for 2017 turned out to be the key to success two years down the road – but we will get to that.

So what was the plan and where were the gaps? In short – I got lost in the specifics and forgot about some of the big picture stuff. The minutiae in a race like this is crucial – but they serve a purpose, they shape the plan, they give texture to the details like food, pace, load, and they give us the executables. The big picture stuff, often the intangibles, are what we must be able to call upon to allow us to execute the plan. I looked at the specifics – load, pace, calories – but I didn't give enough attention to what it was going to take to have the discipline, the resilience, the sheer grit that would be required to keep me in the game, level-headed and delivering – hour after hour, day after day, kilometre after kilometre.

Now that's not to say I slacked off, far from it. I looked at the race from three perspectives – cold weather management, physical and mental prep, and logistics.

COLD WEATHER MANAGEMENT

This is the aspect that I was most comfortable with. After years of high altitude climbing, hanging out in tents on frozen mountain sides, dragging sleds across glaciers, I knew what I was in for. Doesn't make it any less painful or dangerous but I felt well equipped to monitor for warning signs and knew that I had the prerequisite gear to allow my little 70kg frame to stay 'not-frozen' as opposed to being particularly 'warm'.

For people who haven't experienced true, long cold exposure before, it's a little tricky to explain. There is the initial shock which, for me at least, seems to subside fairly quickly. Then there is the slow, insidious seeping of those frozen tendrils into your muscles and bones, draining precious energy and forcing the body to work harder and harder just to maintain any form of equilibrium. Dexterity is limited, either because you're working while wearing bulky gloves or mittens, or alternatively because in either frustration or desperation you take them off and suddenly your fingers are no longer functioning as they used to – slow, clumsy, uncooperative. Then you have the task of getting those gloves back on and reversing their state, unlocking those capillaries and driving warm blood back out to numb and stark-white extremities. And all of that is without the added 'bonus' of dealing with the wind. When that wind swirls up or – as it does across the Dempster – slams into you with all the subtlety of a sumo wrestler, that's when the blades are out. Like a thousand knives relentlessly slashing any exposed skin while simultaneously hammering away at your layers of clothes, leeching out any hard earned warmth within. It is a non-stop barrage that cannot be reasoned or negotiated with. There is only the battle against a tireless foe. What can I tell you – it's a blast.

Getting some extra and more importantly, suitable, cold weather experience in Australia was almost impossible. The best I could manage was a marathon at Falls Creek at the tail end of the ski season – a full marathon in the snow, with temperatures around the -5C. In addition to that I practised my sleep system – set up and pack up – with gloves on, trying to refine the process and eliminate excess steps to get total time down to as little as possible.

PHYSICAL AND MENTAL PREP

This is where the sweat happens. My theory was to establish a rock solid base of GPP (general physical preparedness) to provide a strong and mobile body, ready to do the work. Getting access to a gym, not a problem – I owned one! I had been a CrossFit Affiliate owner for six years; I had the full spectrum of fun 'toys' to work with to make sure I would be ready to roll. Rather than spend time programming myself (it's not my strong point) I paid for a general program from a coach I respect and admire (and still do) and supplemented with additional running and sled work. I should clarify – by sled work I mean an indoor steel sled (often referred to as a prowler) loaded with weight plates – pushed and pulled along a forty metre strip of artificial turf, lap after lap after lap after lap, often for hours at a time.

A standard training week was two sessions per day four days a week, two single-session days and a rest day. The 'two-a-days' were strength focus for one session and conditioning for the other. The single days were conditioning only. As the months ticked down I scaled back the raw strength work and increased the conditioning work, going longer and longer as the race got closer and closer.

The mental prep work was far less structured – I simply got used to 'suffering' in the athletic sense. Not so much in the style of red-lining and spending time in the hole, more the aspect of being tired and sore but still having to put in the work. Getting comfortable with dragging a sled for hours on end, trying to find the capacity to drop into a quiet mental state as I worked through long grinds. What was missing was purpose – as the adage goes, 'are you getting the adaptation you want or are you just getting better at suffering?'. The truth was I was getting good at suffering but that wasn't necessarily the adaptation I needed. Unfortunately for me, I didn't have a clear picture of what adaptation I did need. That knowledge would come much later, after a painful but highly educational experience.

A few months before the race, my sled arrived. Direct from the UK to me – I remember unwrapping it with my eldest son, Campbell, relishing every new piece, daydreaming about all manner of experiences that this sled and I would see. Having the sled early and at home served dual purposes – I could plan out the logistics of how it would be packed and organised for the race – and it allowed me to spend some time 'in the harness', actually dragging the sled around. The term 'dragging' isn't really appropriate as it did have four small detachable wheels. The theory being that while on the road you would use the wheels but once we transitioned onto the frozen rivers and working on ice, we had the option of removing the wheels and letting the sled slide.

My last piece of training kit was a trusty old car tyre. With a rope secured to it and attached to my harness, I could emulate the sled drag with the additional resistance and friction the tyre provided. My driveway became my tyre-drag lap ground, much to my dogs' joy as they followed me up and down, lap after lap (to put this in context, a lap of our driveway is about 300m, it's a decent country driveway).

LOGISTICS

Lastly came the logistics – equipment, nutrition and pace.

Equipment was a tricky one – I had the vast majority of what I needed as a result of previous expeditions. The question was how much was enough? You don't want to be dragging unnecessary weight, but you don't want to risk running out or missing a crucial piece of kit that could make the difference between finishing or failing. The sleds themselves had an optional bag that was designed to fit the full length, giving you one large internal space. I had chosen to forgo that for economic reasons, that and the fact that I had accumulated piles of bags, duffels and backpacks in the garage over the years – surely I could rig up some options out of all of those!

The race organisers had provided a mandatory gear list but it was surprisingly spartan – it was 'mandatory' and the remainder was left open to athletic choice and interpretation. Sleeping bag (rated to -40C), clothing suitable for -40C, capability to cover all exposed skin from head to toe, stove and fuel suitable for melting snow, head torch for nights. That was about it in the 'mandatory' department. After that ran a long list of suggested gear – thermals, shoes, balaclavas, gloves, liners, mitts. Then there was all the food and capacity to carry water – and not just a sufficient volume of water but in a manner that would delay its inevitable freezing for as long as possible. You had the means of getting more water – just set up the stove and melt snow/ice. The problem was that this was not only a massive pain in the butt, it was unbelievably time consuming. You had to stop, set up, pray that your stove would light (the fuel was often so cold it simply would not light) and then sit there slowly freezing yourself while you waited to get enough water. If there was any way to avoid stopping to get the stove going, you would take it. In my mind the stove was the absolute last resort – I would rather carry an extra 500g–1kg of water weight in the sled than risk a long stop to produce that amount. The challenge from a clothing perspective was layering – you couldn't simply have a few thick layers, especially when it came to hands. Layers allow you to regulate temperature quickly and efficiently – which was crucial. Too hot (too many layers) and you start to sweat, stop for a minute to organise some gear or get some food and that sweat freezes and suddenly you're not only covered in ice, but have a wet layer next to you, a sure-fire recipe for hypothermia and disaster. Too cold (too few layers) and it's either put more layers on or get into your sleeping bag, they are literally the only too significant ways you can warm up. Sure you can pick up the pace and try to get the blood pumping but reality is that's only a short term solution if the weather doesn't improve, especially if you cannot maintain that increased pace for very long. You have to be realistic and have solid solutions for race-ending and potentially life-threatening situations like hypothermia.

Having a system to keep your hands warm is an art form. You have to balance the need for dexterity in certain situations – eating, adjusting equipment like your harness – without putting your digits at risk. Fingers present a particular risk for frostbite, the capillaries, especially if they are not accustomed to it, will quickly shut down in a bid to direct warmth back towards the body core. The cold sensation in the fingertips quickly progresses to numbness and telltale white colour as the capillaries clamp down and the interstitial fluid begins to freeze and crystallise. Dexterity disappears and suddenly you are well on your way to getting frostbite. The key once again was layers. I worked on a system of light liner, followed by a mid-weight fleece glove and then the option of a heavy weight glove or mitt. The glove left you with some degree of dexterity but cost you some degree of warmth. The mitts sacrificed the use of individual fingers to execute tasks but were much warmer – the entire hand could be clasped together inside the core of the mitt to retain warmth and circulation.

A similar scenario applied for headwear – light buffs, heavier beanies and eventually full, heavy-weight balaclavas. There was also the issue of your neck and breath. Often overlooked is the effect of such extreme cold air on your respiration and fluid requirements. The nasal passages would often freeze up very quickly – they would respond to the cold by pushing fluid into the capillaries and sinuses which would eventually somewhat freeze up, leaving you with a fairly permanently blocked nose. That meant breathing though your mouth, which doesn't sound much of a problem until you understand some of the biomechanical short cuts you're now taking. The nasal passages serve multiple purposes, one of which is slightly warming the incoming air before it descends into the lungs. Bypass the nose and the heating system gets turned off – that incredibly dry and cold air is on an express lane from the Arctic direct to your lungs. On the way out, the air is carrying an increased degree of moisture as it tries to mitigate that damage of the dry air coming in, so now you're not only getting rid of carbon dioxide but you're also handing off far more fluid than you may be used too – an insidious and often overlooked contributor to dehydration.

To mitigate all of that, racers take one of two approaches – using light-to-medium weight buffs to pull up from the neck over the nose and mouth or using a more robust approach such as face mask, like a 'cold avenger' mask. Both have their pros and cons. The buffs would trap the outgoing moisture on your breath and would quickly freeze and go from being soft flexible material to having the yoga capabilities of corrugated iron. The full masks were effective but could feel slightly claustrophobic, and they trapped all the moisture, often leaving you with pools of fluid gathering in the mask. In the end, I chose the buff route and made sure I had plenty of them.

I will spare you the no doubt fascinating details of my selection of boxers, long johns and thermal pants. Needless to say – layers, layers, layers. My last resort for lower body layering was what I referred to as my 'nuclear option' – when it all goes to hell – they were bulky down pants, imagine a pair of pants made out of your doona, covered in windproof material and all held up with a good 'ole pair of braces – very fetching!

Nutrition – you have to fuel the machine. You can't go on these types of races or expeditions and expect to 'enjoy' the food. You have to make peace with the fact that it's not food – it's just fuel. I decided to enlist the help of a sports nutritionist – I had a contact who came highly recommended and had experience with fuelling for extreme length events. After some back and forth we developed a plan around not only how much I needed to consume but even down to what that would be. We calculated calories in based on twelve-hour blocks, broke that down into individual meals, and macronutrients. From there I could figure out how much food I would need with me on the sled and how much in the two drop bags we had access to along the way. The theory was bulletproof and the planning was meticulous…only two 'little snags'. The first I would discover on arrival in Canada, the second I would discover about 12 hours into the race. We'll address each of those in due course – suffice to say, the plan looked beautiful when I printed it out on paper. Best laid plans…

The last piece of the puzzle – at least pre-race – was pacing. Just how long would all this take? Not so much from a big picture perspective – I knew there was a gross overall time limit of 191 hours, but more from a point-to-point perspective. Checkpoints were anywhere from 70km to 120km apart, so judging how much food and water you would need between was obviously entirely dependent on how long you thought it would take to get from A to B. Luckily athletes had access to race data from previous years – every athlete, each year, their time in and out of each checkpoint and alongside all of that the inevitable and staggering wave of yellow blocks on the spreadsheet with the word 'WITHDRAWN' embalmed in the middle. From all of that I could put my 'nerd powers' to good use – a quick home-made spreadsheet later and I had the average pace of each athlete from checkpoint to checkpoint. I then estimated what I would do based off of that data – another of the many critical mistakes I would make. What I should have done was figure out what I was capable of and then plan based on my real capacity as opposed to thinking, 'sure I can keep up with that pace, I'll do that'. In the comfort of my warm office, all these numbers seem entirely reasonable, almost comfortable, compared to my regular race pace.

I reflect now on the planning and prep I did for my 2017 attempt, with the wisdom of hindsight and the advantage of the months and years of reflection post. I can see quite clearly why I thought I had a solid plan, why I came to the conclusions I did regarding load, pace, nutrition, expectations – the whole deal. Logic dictated that I was correct, that my assumptions were valid and that I could have a very reasonable expectation of the race not only going to plan, but of me returning three weeks after departure with a resolute 'mission accomplished' stamped in the passport.

The real world, this race, my body and mind – would all conspire to deliver a very different experience.

CHAPTER 5
Only 14,000km to go

Warrnambool, Australia to
Whitehorse, Canada.
March 2017

WARRNAMBOOL TO WHITEHORSE isn't exactly a walk in the park when it comes to travel. I have a long-suffering travel agent who for years has had the 'pleasure' of me walking through his doors and announcing that I need him to find a way to get me from sunny regional Warrnambool, tucked away in the southwest corner of Victoria, Australia – to some far flung flyspeck of a town in a remote and often unheard of part of the world. The kind of places where he has to figure out if they even have an airport, let alone the booking code.

Turns out Warrnambool to Whitehorse was a thirty-hour grind of flights and layovers. Three-hour drive, Warrnambool to Melbourne, our nearest major airport. Two-hour flight from Melbourne to Brisbane – sunny Brisbane, a glorious 29C when

I boarded my Air Canada flight to Vancouver. A few hours in Brisbane, thirteen hours jammed in a plane seat to Vancouver, the joy of working your way through customs while jet lagged and overloaded on airline food, a further five hours uncomfortably jammed into a random airport seat drifting in and out of something that has a passing resemblance to sleep, only to find that your flight to Whitehorse has finally been delayed by a further four hours. Eventually you shuffle your zombie-like corpse onto the plane for the last few hours up to Whitehorse. You step off and outside, the first time you've breathed fresh air since Brisbane, only to find that the fresh air here is a brisk -20C. That's how you fix jet lag – get off a warm plane, step outside and freeze. A veritable Arctic slap across the face – highly effective and somewhat invigorating.

Thankfully my gear arrived – a few athletes were hanging in the terminal having arrived days earlier with nervous faces, hoping that their delayed luggage (containing all their race gear) would make its long awaited debut on the luggage carousel.

The race director, Martin Like, greeted me at the airport and promptly popped me on the shuttle bus to the hotel. Thirty minutes later and I had officially arrived. Tucked away in my little hotel room, with all equipment and bags – it was Monday morning. The race would start Friday morning.

Tuesday was 'do all the shopping' day. It was here that the first critical error with my nutrition plan would surface. You're not in Kansas anymore…just because your plan was meticulously laid out down to the product didn't mean that your choice of products would be ready and waiting for you on the shiny shelves of your local Whitehorse supermarket. In fact virtually none of it was. I had pre-ordered all my freeze-dried means via email and when I went to collect it, discovered they didn't stock half of what I had planned on. All of a sudden the nutrition plan would be developed on the fly from what was available. I fell back on previous race experience for what I knew would be tolerable and calorie packed – bags of nut mix, Clif bars, freeze-dried meals heavy in carbs. Eating chicken and rice for days on end didn't seem like a big deal. There was also that perverse pleasure of buying an inordinately large amount of food you would never normally buy – this experience occurred pretty much solely in the confectionery aisle. As an athlete this is normally the no-go zone but pre-race you're like a five year old set loose on the goodie table at your first friend's birthday party – it's a free for all. If you are 'fun size', 'double dipped', or a family value pack then please, join your brethren in my now overloaded shopping trolley. Last but not least I grabbed a six pack of meal replacement drink – the kind of product they use for the elderly or post-surgery when you can't eat solids but need the calories. I thought this was a particularly clever move – turns out, not so much, but more on that later.

Tuesday was also race briefing and kit-test day in the afternoon. All the athletes and crew gathered in the meeting room of the High Country Inn. We received our sky-blue, logo-emblazoned, puffy, insulated race jackets and got the low-down on what was to come – to some degree.

This race had no map. No GPS co-ordinates. We put you on the start line, we point you north and say 'go'. Just keep going north – that's what the compass is for – don't go south. (A few chuckles around the room) The chuckles were squashed as Martin informed us that sleep-deprived athletes had been known to stop, set up bivvy for a sleep and on waking forget that they had turned their sled around before bunking down. They got up, harnessed and headed off – in the completely wrong direction… for miles…until a medic crew came past and asked them what the hell they were doing.

If Martin's briefing, while important, was somewhat more on the jovial side, the medics who came next proffered no such levity. The medics were the field-based decision makers – they had final, non-negotiable say on whether you continued or were summarily removed from the race, with or without your consent. One of the medics, Scotty, gave us one of the best pieces of advice I have ever received for an environment such as that waiting for us 'in the north'.

'This environment will disproportionately punish any and every mistake you make.'

Let's put that in perspective. Say you don't tie your shoelace properly (firstly why are you wearing shoelaces when you could have planned ahead and used any quick-lace system? …needless to say I had shoelaces) so your shoelace slowly but surely works itself undone and now you need to tie it. Not exactly a full blown crisis… except to tie your shoelace you need dexterity, which means fingers unencumbered by bulky gloves or mitts – you know, the very things stopping your fingers from becoming the human version of snap-frozen string beans. So you stop (and your body temperature starts to decline as you are no longer moving) you remove gloves/mitts and the clock starts in your head – mere seconds and the dexterity starts to decline, the blood flow starts to retreat – if you don't quite tie it right and fiddle around for those few extra seconds, you now have cold, white fingers. You jam them back in your gloves – and head off at a hard pace trying to get the blood pumping back into the extremities. It doesn't sound like much but I can tell you from painful experience that the mind races as the minutes tick by and you continue to have no feeling in your fingers. Is it coming back? How long will this take? What happens if I need my hands for something critical in those next few minutes? You frantically open and close your hands, walk hard and pray for those first painful tingles as the blood pushes its way into capillaries that have been slammed shut. And that was just one of the myriad issues that require a free and flexible hand – wait till you need to open a tricky freeze-dried packet, or need to go to the toilet, or your harness strap unravels and slips out of its clasp and needs to be re-fed through for the tenth time. Or best of all, wait until one of the wheels on your sled has a serious malfunction and you find yourself trail-side, sled inverted, trying to use small metal hand tools and a few zip-ties to try and MacGyver it all back into some sort of working order.

So we receive the obligatory warnings around hypothermia, where to sleep safely, the importance of self-care for blisters, exposed skin, dealing with sweating, not dehydrating and last but not least… chafing. Yep, good ol' chafing. Sounds like a pretty innocuous and somewhat embarrassing issue but many a racer had been removed from the race, or was simply unable to continue, due to suffering from what could only be described as a 'biblical level of chafing'. So get that anti-chafe cream folks and layer it on those sensitive areas like your life (and buttocks) depends on it.

The last task for Tuesday afternoon was the compulsory test

run for first-time athletes. Returning athletes (who comprised the majority of the field) were welcome to come along but were free to choose. So early afternoon we all awkwardly manhandle our loaded sleds down through hotel elevators, hallways and stairs to assemble outside, harness up and head off along the river for a two-hour 'dry-run'. A few hours later the medics call a stop and ask everyone to set up their bivvy (or sleep system – a few people had opted for one-man tents as opposed to the low-lying swag) as well as get your stove out, light it and make a cup of tea. This was their way of ensuring that if worst came to worst, all athletes could organise shelter and get a warm drink happening in the case that they needed to bunker down and face a long wait for help to arrive. I was confident going into this – I had practised this exact drill multiple times at home – I was not confident coming out of it.

By the time I had got my sleeping kit out of my sled bag – sleeping bag, two sleeping mats and swag – the athlete next to me (Matt, another Aussie) had his swag out, laid out and was tucked in snug. I hadn't even started to get everything laid out, let alone get myself into it. I was slow – this was, unfortunately, news to me. It was a logistics problem – I had pretty much the same components as everyone else, they just had it all pre-setup, rolled up and jammed back into their large sled bag. I had opted for two mid-sized bags, one for gear and one for food/fuel/water. All had made sense to me except that I didn't really have room for a fully made-up swag rolled up, I had to compress down and pack my sleeping bag every time as well as fold up my mats and store them on the outside of my sled bags. Rookie mistakes…so many rookie mistakes.

The next boondoggle was my stove – it would start up just fine in the sunny confines of my backyard at home. Here in the pristine chill of -20C Whitehorse, the winter mix fuel was so cold it simply flat-out refused to light and as match after burnt-out match piled up beside me, one of the medics sidled up and asked, 'How's that stove going?' Not embarrassing at all – his advice was two-fold, warm up your fuel before you try to use it (that meant getting it out and jamming it down your top for fifteen to twenty minutes before you want to use it) and make sure you have a lot of matches. That last 'pearl of wisdom' delivered with a wry smile.

The last 'kicker' of this little dry-run was the inordinate amount of 'gear-envy' and mild panic it could induce. Everyone was doing those little sideway glances at the person next to them, what gear did they have, what little gadget or cool piece of equipment that I clearly didn't have. The FOMO was very real, culminating in most athletes making a last minute dash down the main street of Whitehorse to panic buy a bunch of kit before we headed off for the two day drive to the start line. By the time our convoy pulled out the next morning I'm fairly certainly there wasn't a windproof match, hand warmer or energy bar left for sale anywhere in the greater city of Whitehorse – we had picked them clean.

The drive to the start line was two very long days, jammed packed like sardines into a convoy of ubiquitous black GMC Suburbans, heading north to the start line at Eagle Plains. Only two things of any note occurred on the way – the greatest cinnamon buns in the world and a shot of whiskey with a dead-man's toe in it.

The cinnamon buns were at a place called Braeburn Lodge, a little log style cabin tucked away on the side of the highway, a checkpoint in the famed Yukon Quest. The faded and peeling signboard outside advised that they were 'world famous' for their cinnamon buns. In what may be a marketing first – it was a claim that was entirely justified. Made to order on site and delivered piping hot to your table, a single cinnamon bun was roughly the size of a human head. They were monumental. Essentially a one-way ticket to type-two diabetes delivered on a plate with a side of aluminium foil as no one ever finished them, the sizeable remains were always taken – probably to sustain a family of four for days.

The other experience was the Sourtoe Cocktail. (You can google this if you wish but I assure you – it's a thing.) It works like this – in the old frontier town of Dawson, our overnight stop, there is a pub. And that pub has the somewhat unfathomable claim to fame that the locals will bequeath their toes (yes those digits at the end of your feet) in their wills, to the pub. Suitably preserved, the toes awaited travellers (such as us) to order and 'experience' a Sourtoe Cocktail. A shot of Yukon Jack whiskey is poured and into said whiskey, the preserved toe is unceremoniously 'dropped' with the instruction that, 'You can drink it fast, or drink it slow, but the lips must touch the toe.'

The head gets tipped back, the whiskey goes down and sure enough, your lips make contact with a shrivelled, preserved, whiskey-soaked human toe. (Which to add insult to injury, has been busy touching the lips of all the other race participants and who knows who-else all evening. You get a certificate (which I still have), a round of applause and the toe gets fished out of the bottom of the glass ready for another journey. I kid you not.

Finally we arrived at the Eagle Plains roadhouse, which was perched on the side of the Dempster Highway – a road made famous outside of the reaches of far northern Canada by the show 'Ice Road Truckers'. The roadhouse itself is two-thirds frontier, one third Stephen King novel. Staffed by a small group of family members, with walls adorned by old black and white prints from a bygone era – trappers, frontiersmen, indigenous inhabitants all staring down from the walls of the hallway as we stalk past. A weird combination of the cold, the air pressure and the lack of humidity means the entire building seems to resonate with the low-level hum of pent-up static electricity. Whenever you go to place your key (an actual physical metal key) into the lock (no swipe cards here) you are reminded of its presence by the arc of blue light that leaps from door handle to key and into your hand. The dining room is watched over by wall-mounted caribou heads, magnificent antlers and the odd bear pelt. It's quirky in a magnificent way.

A final dinner, the flurry of last minute packing, unpacking and repacking, gear sorting, final messages home (via what seemed to be the world's slowest and most intermittent internet connection) and a fitful sleep awaiting the dawn of race day. Over the last six days I've travelled over 14,000km, gone from temperatures as high as 29C to as low as -20C and eaten everything from appalling aircraft food to juicy bison steaks. And finally we are at the start line ready to see what is in store for this motley crew of intrepid adventurers.

And so it begins.

CHAPTER 6

All roads lead to Fort Mac

Eagle Plains to Fort McPherson
Yukon, Northwest Territories, Canada
March 2017

Three…two…one…GO.

It was the most unceremonious start to an enormous race. The start was given by one of the local road workers – the road we were about to head out on was regularly and impassably swamped by massive snow drifts, driven by winds strong enough to blow fully laden trucks clean off the road. Crews tasked with both keeping the road clear and pulling out snow-bound trucks were a regular feature. The guy looked at the twenty-three of us assembled at the start as though we were all mad.

'Good luck. Um. Go?'

And with that we were off.

It's a strange feeling, that big adrenaline dump that comes with 'go' – a typical response to the start of a race, but with a race so long, that adrenaline is going to be long gone and you'll still have 99% of the distance to cover. The excitement and enthusiasm that came with those first kilometres would be quickly tempered, leaving only me, my sled and my thoughts as the kilometres piled up and the enormity of the task ahead began making itself painfully known.

We had been 'advised' that the terrain was 'a little hilly' at the start. What that translated to was that over the first 115km we would approach, scale and pass over the Richardson Mountain range. Minor detail.

The first checkpoint is on the line of latitude that designates the Arctic Circle, marking our official transition across the line that separates the domain of the northern end of the Earth from basically, everything else. Checkpoint 1 (CP1) was 36km from the start line and was a fairly innocuous start. I say innocuous but that is the best part of a marathon before you reach the first checkpoint, and it's still the shortest section of the race by a very wide margin. A long, slow descent down to Engineer Creek and then the slow climb back up. Rolling hills and some sweeping bends, the wide expanse of the snow and sparse, stunted vegetation that marked the Yukon stretched out either side of us. Already my lack of a coherent pacing plan was delivering some mental anguish – everyone had taken off like a rocket, suddenly it seemed like everyone was in a mad rush, running. I remember jogging along, swept up in it all and asking Tom, the athlete next to me, 'Why the hell are we running?'

I had started at the front of the field, not by design, I'd just got to the start line before the bulk of the field. Now as we ascended some of the early hills, other athletes were passing me – not in a speed-goat kind of a way but more in a gradual, 'you've got a longer stride and faster cadence than me' kind of way. Every time someone passed me that little voice in the back of my head piped up wondering if I was too slow, too unprepared, heading for the back of the field already. It was all nonsense. Logically I knew that within half a day we would be so spread out that we would have virtually no idea where anyone was let alone any idea how fast or slow they were going. Still, I managed to concern myself with nonsensical details of whether the person behind me was catching me or not – as if it mattered.

CP1 – filled up my couple of thermos flasks, made up a freeze-dried meal and ate it sitting in the stone cold, cramped and packed trailer that was CP1. Sorted some gear out in my sled as I prepared to tackle my first night racing in the Arctic. All in all, I was at that checkpoint for the better part of an hour. To put that in perspective, two years later I would spend the sum total of roughly eight minutes there.

I'd had this romantic notion about how the nights would be on the race. In my mind it would be the very pinnacle of a great adventure – charging forth, solo, deep into the Arctic night, my head torch a solitary beam of white light beneath a sky laden with the green ebb and flow of the northern lights. Bear Grylls eat your heart out.

My experience that night turned out to be as far removed from such a fanciful dream as to be comical. The sun sank below the horizon and with it the last vestiges of warmth, real or imagined. The temperature plummeted deep into the -30C. The cold was nothing short of brutal. It was pervasive and relentless, there was simply no respite. You couldn't call the ref and grab a five-minute time-out.

There was nowhere to stop and shelter – as darkness enveloped everything, my entire world was reduced to the feeble circle of white light thrown out by my ice-encrusted head torch (the batteries for which were tucked away under all my clothing in a bid to keep them warm and functioning – the cold literally sucks the life clean out of them). Already the race was beginning to claim 'victims' and the 'withdrawn' title was starting to make itself known. For some it was strategic errors – went too hard, got sweaty and didn't have sufficient dry clothes to change into – race over. For others it was finding themselves trapped between the psychological anvil of the dawning realisation that this was only the first night of many and the hammer blow of the bone-cracking cold. My romantic notions of adventure in the Arctic had been unceremoniously slapped out of me.

I reached the Rock River campground in the very dark and early hours of the morning. This was an unofficial checkpoint that several athletes had mentioned they would grab some sleep at on the first night. One of the checkpoint trailers was parked here and you could grab some hot water – if it was available. I had discovered over the last few hours that the cold meant keeping a thick buff pulled up over my mouth and nose to fend off getting a frostbitten nose, what that translated to was the warmer air coming from my mouth being directed upward straight onto the cold glass of my spectacles (I'm very short sighted) which immediately fogged them up. No manner of adjusting and fiddling seemed to alleviate the problem. In the end I had simply removed my glasses and was walking along the road with everything well out of focus – so much so that I almost missed the slight trail to the left towards the campground.

There were bivvies and swags set out on the narrow trail beside where the trailer was parked, so I decided to follow their lead and set about pitching my sleeping swag. After fiddling about with setting out my mat, inflating a second mat for insulation and finally shuffling into my sleeping bag I was cold to the point of shivering. Some time after the race a fellow competitor and now great friend, Pete, pointed out the bleeding obvious, which is that the Rock River Campground is at the lowest point of the entire first few days of the course – is it literally the precise point where all the cold air descends to and sits. It's a deep freezer within a freezer and here was a bunch of us who had decided that this looked like a pretty good place to try and sleep and warm up. Geniuses.

Roughly ninety minutes later – virtually all of it spent shivering in my bag I gave up, got up, packed up and set off again towards the coming dawn and the daunting prospect of climbing and getting over the infamous Wrights Pass. All in all, I had wasted the best part of two hours, made zero progress and only had bone-chilling cold to show for it.

Dawn.

The sun rose to find me slowly working my way towards the last major climb up to Wrights Pass.

'Trucks use low gear, steep climb.' All the usual motivational signposts appeared on the roadside. It was 7am and my legs were as heavy as my eyelids – not even a full day into the race. My sled felt like it weighed a ton as I trudged my way up the endless sweeps and bends that composed the final non-stop seven-kilometre climb to the Pass. Several times I had to stop and take a moment to shake out the legs and mentally take a few breaths.

Wrights Pass had been described to us as 'Hurricane Alley'. As I approached the top demarcated by a signposted lookout carpark, a small car approached me, slowed and the window came down. A guy leaned out and informed me that, 'It's a bit windy on the other side'. Turns out he had an undeniable skill for a biblical level of understatement.

Cross the few, gently undulating rises and falls at the top of the Pass and then down we go. You could hear it before you felt it. Like a deity-sized steam train bearing down, from behind the mountains, gathering speed before cutting through the exposed pass on my left and slamming into all and sundry. All thoughts of anything 'race' were literally swept from my mind. It was all I could do to stay on my feet. I was 'buttoned up' – heavy jacket fully zipped, every square centimetre of skin covered and protected, all focus on placing one foot in front of the other and moving forward, not sideways. On a positive note, I remember thinking – well at least I'm getting a true Arctic experience. I think some part of me would have been disappointed if Hurricane Alley had let me pass unscathed. It wasn't without victims, a momentary lapse in grip saw one athlete's heavy down jacket liberated from his hand and sent hurtling away over the tundra. Race over – no longer in possession of a critical piece of mandatory gear. All that training, prep, equipment, hopes and dreams vanished in an instant with the smallest lapse in concentration. A reminder that this environment would punish – everything, all the time, without remorse, fear or favour. Hurricane Alley felt like it lasted for hours when in fact we were probably only exposed to the worst of it for around 60 minutes. From there we rounded onto the lee side and continued the slow grind along the excoriated gravel of the Dempster toward Checkpoint 2 – James Creek Depot.

It was mid-afternoon on the second day when I dragged myself into James Creek – council depot that housed major road-clearing equipment in a huge work shed, with a few stand-alone cabins to house workers. Snow drifts had piled themselves high against every building. We were permitted to go into the massive garage to get some shelter and potentially try to sleep – with the minor detail that this was a functioning and busy depot, so the radio was on, CB was on, air thick with diesel fumes and the only spot to lie down was on the oil-stained concrete workshop floor. A cacophony of noise above, stone hard concrete below.

I remember this CP really well – because of the mental and emotional turmoil I found myself in. I took a quick picture on my phone and when I show it to people I describe it as the most honest selfie ever taken. I look windswept, battered and shaken. Which is entirely accurate. My experience of the night before had left me emotionally and physically bruised and shocked. This was the first night, of maybe a week's worth of nights, each getting more and more remote and potentially colder and colder. Everything ached, I was already hours behind the time I thought I would arrive, courtesy of hours spent fumbling around at Rock River and being far slower than I thought I would be climbing up and over Wrights Pass. I was 114km into a 583km race and was already feeling broken and lost.

Tim Hamlin – another Aussie athlete (there was three other Australians racing – Tim, Matt and me in the full-length 584km race and Bronwyn in the shorter course 193km race) called out to me, asking when I was planning on heading back out.

I told him I didn't know.

What do you mean you don't know?

I don't know if I can.

It was at that moment, verbalising that fact that I realised I was truly scared. The thought of heading out again, into a second night that was getting closer and closer simply filled me with dread. Tim pulled me out of a dark moment that may well have ended my race there and then had it not been for his support.

'Let's go together, it's not a race mate it's just about survival. I've got a thermos of hot choc, you've got one of coffee. Let's go together.'

While that moment probably was nothing special for Tim, he would've helped anyone at any time regardless, it changed my future. If I had folded then and pulled out, I would have gone home, shattered, disappointed, never to return. He got me up, out and back on the road and even though the end result for this race would be the same, he got me back in the game and gave me the chance to push almost 200km further into the race, gaining knowledge, understanding and what would eventually come to me as confidence two years later. I thank my lucky stars for that discussion and his support every day.

By the time we packed up, ate, refilled our thermos and started heading off, night had descended once more. The good news was that the hills were about to give way to long sweeps of gentle undulation. When I say 'long' we were looking at almost 300km or more of vast, flat, remote wilderness. We headed out and the company of another human, trapped in a similar race hell to me, made a monumental difference. We chatted about anything and everything as the kilometres ticked by. At one point Tim's sled decided that it wasn't going to play the game anymore – one of the wheels 'liberated' itself from the axle and staged an impromptu stop-work meeting. Looking back now it was almost comical, a true Arctic MacGyver moment as the two of us, armed with little more than a multi-tool and some zip ties attempted, successfully I might add, to re-affix the wheel and get us back moving again.

As the early hours greeted us, we decided to bivvy up on the side of the road. It was literally a comedy. It was the first time on the race Tim had set up his bivvy and it wasn't entirely going to plan. He's a talkative bloke and for the best part of about an hour and half he talked, muttered, questioned and generally made noise while I was trying to sleep literally right next to him. We managed some sleep but eventually decided to call it quits, get up and get moving.

Tim, like a vast majority of the population, is taller than me. So naturally he has a slightly longer stride than me so eventually as the kilometres accumulated we started to drift apart. We hadn't set an agreement in stone to stick together it was simply smart and convenient coming out of James Creek but now as we worked our way to Fort McPherson we had slowly but surely drifted apart, Tim well ahead.

Coming towards Fort Mac you cross the Peel River at a ferry station – a spot frozen over – complete with the requisite ice-locked ferries sitting there in mute disapproval of your performance. The trail seemed really unclear here, especially to my heavily sleep-deprived eyes and exhausted mind. I started to seriously doubt that I was in the right place, had I fallen asleep on my feet and missed a turn (which was completely plausible)? Was I lost?

Surely I must be close, I felt that Fort Mac should have appeared any moment, it couldn't be that far away surely? I decided to move on up the trail for another kilometre to two in the hopes of spotting a sign that might set my mind at ease. I found the sign but the comfort was short lived. I was indeed on the right road and Fort McPherson was indeed ahead – only it was still 11km away, not the measly one or two I had hoped. It was soul crushing. In the warmth of your home, or the comfort of your weekend, walking along the beach 11km may not sound like much, but this was effectively a sign that said I was at least three hours away from the next checkpoint. It was bitterly cold down here on the river and I wasn't getting out of this anytime soon. Happy travels. Tim later admitted to me that on seeing that exact sign he stopped, sat down and cried.

The final stretch of road into Fort Mac is a cruel and sadistic joke. The sign welcoming you is posted an almost comically large distance away from the town itself, delivering a mock sense of false hope to the weary bodies slowly dragging their sled through the now heavy snow. It winds and winds and slowly rises and falls. Each time you reach a small crest, you're certain you will see the town laid out before you, only to be met with yet more hills and more road and more snow and no town. I finally turned into Fort Mac, making the long trudge up the single main street to the checkpoint, a community centre that afforded us a warm indoor gymnasium to sleep in, a kitchen and the absurd and incomprehensible luxury of a functioning toilet – that was inside, and clean, and you could actually sit on.

As I got to the front steps, Michael Hull (Hully), one of the support crew, came out to grab my 98 bags off my sled to bring them inside. A chance to sort gear, collect the first of two drop bags and resupply. As he picked up my bag he exclaimed, 'My God how much have you got in here?' Well that's awkward. I didn't know exactly, but based on that critique I'll go with, 'too much'.

I found a spot tucked away in the gym and laid out my mats and sleeping bag, Hully asked me how long I wanted to sleep for, he was keeping a chart and would wake us up when requested, sparing us the disaster of dropping into a deep sleep for far more hours than we could afford. Three hours was my answer. It was the most I could squeeze in and far less than I wanted.

Anyone who has endured a hard and long race will testify to the fact that despite an often epic level of tiredness, sleep isn't always as forthcoming as you would expect. In fact, it can be downright elusive. Hours of elevated heart rate and adrenaline, coupled with cramped and fatigued muscles and a mind racing after long hours of diligence all conspire to ensure that real restorative sleep remains nothing more than a fantasy. You garner a few restless hours of something that approximates sleep and leaves you refreshed enough to get up and get moving but with nothing that even begins to repair or reduce the damage that has been done. Hully dutifully woke me, I chowed down another freeze-dried meal and made preparations to head off to Checkpoint 4 at Tsiigetchic. As I was about to leave, Jamie, one of the medics pulled me aside and gave me the hard word. We had been told in the original briefing, eons ago in the comfort of Whitehorse, that if you were not out of Fort Mac by midnight on Sunday you were well and truly stacking the odds against your chance of finishing the race before official cut-off at 9am the following Saturday. I was heading out at 11.30pm.

'Listen – you have to motor. Head down and go. I want three hours hard graft, stop for fifteen, eat and then another three hours hard. This is how it has to be.'

He was right. He wasn't trying to act tough or demoralise me – it was simply the truth. I was slow and the clock was ticking. And I had a bloody long way to go. I took it both as a warning and a motivator. Let's go.

I clipped on my harness, sled falling into place behind me, and instantly got lost. One of the support crew, Murray, had said to follow him out as he drove ahead to show the way out of town. I had stopped for a moment to look down and fix something and when I looked up, he had vanished. Around a corner no doubt but in the dark I simply could not find him. I felt like an absolute fool – I was lost in an almost literal one-street town. In the end I asked a local walking past which way to the road to Tsiig, he showed me and sure enough as I rounded a corner there was Murray chilling out in his black Suburban. He laughed, smiled and said, 'Walk around that truck parked there, and go straight, for 70km and then boom, you'll be in Tsiigetchic'. Just like that, like it was easy.

I took Jamie's words to heart and charged hard for three hours. I actually started to feel good, I had a cracking pace finally. Up until that point I had been averaging around 4kmph which sounds incredibly slow but keep in mind, that's dragging a sled, in snow, over a mountain pass. Now I was back closer to 6kmph, the kilometres ticked past, as did the time.

I hit the three-hour mark, pulled across to the side of the road and sat down for a drink and some food.

On the food thing – I mentioned that there were two problems with my food plan. The first was that all the products I had planned on at home weren't necessarily available here in Canada so swathes of alterations had to be made. The second was something I simply hadn't thought of but on reflection was blazingly obvious. Take a simple Clif Bar, a favourite of mine, 250cals neatly packed up and ready to roll , one problem – after spending any time whatsoever in my sled, which is attached to me, outside, in -30C and it had become a veritable house brick. Solid as a slab of granite. You couldn't chew it or break it into pieces. I could have used it as foundation for a building raised in honour of my stupidity, but that was about it. So now if I wanted to eat food I had to fish it out of the sled bag, slip it under my clothes, close to my body, for long enough to literally defrost it. If that sounds annoying imagine how damn frustrating that is when you have only slept for a mere few hours in the preceding three days. Patience was running very thin.

I got up and headed off again, determined to follow the three-hour hard graft plan. It was in those next three hours that the cumulative toll of the myriad mistakes I had made would all come home to roost.

This was literally the beginning of the end.

CHAPTER 7
I'm not OK with this

Tsiigetchic, Tuktoyaktuk, Whitehorse
Northwest Territories, Yukon, Canada
March 2017

ON PAPER THIS SECTION WAS the most straightforward of the lot. It was the second shortest in terms of physical distance, relatively flat and generally pretty straight. The 57km from the outskirts of Fort Mac to Tsiig would be my physical undoing, a mental unravelling and witness to the delivery of some undeniable and indelible truths.

I was into the second three-hour block as prescribed by Jamie. In the distance I could see a flashing red light, perched at the top of some kind of mining rig. It looked like it wasn't overly far from me, but we had been warned – that light would mockingly glare at us for the vast majority of this section, helping add to the distortion of distance and time as it seemed to sit unmoving in the distance. Sleep deprivation and physical deterioration joining the party to add to the mental fog that made the mystery of that damn unmoving light almost incomprehensible.

About an hour into that second block and my pace began to falter. My middle back was cramping and seizing as it started to fight back against the previous endless days of being slightly hunched and loaded as I fought forward and the sled dragged along for the ride behind me. In an attempt to alleviate the pain, I would stop, lean forward as if trying to touch my toes, to try to 'unload' it. The plan was to do that for 30 seconds and then straighten up and move on. The only flaw in that plan was that tiny problem of constantly, and almost instantly, falling asleep every time I tried to 'unload'. I would stop, start counting aloud 1…2…3…………..8…9…10. A quick check of my watch would reveal that my ten count had taken about ten minutes, not ten seconds. As the pace slowed the mind started to wander. In the dead of night the hallucinations moved from something I was cognisant of to something I was fully immersed in. I had total belief in the fantasy world my mind was constructing. A few instances stand out that I can remember, and one that I can't.

The one that I can't was actually a drive-by visit from the medics. Apparently they had a brief conversation with me, to them I seemed extremely tired but still, amazingly, able to hold a conversation. At one point they did ask me if I was asleep – to which I replied, 'I think so...' I have no recollection of the conversation whatsoever.

At one point the road suddenly seemed to spring up vertically in front of me, forming a wall that appeared to be literally sky-high. I stopped in my tracks, fearful of actually walking into this non-existent wall. I was perplexed – where did the wall come from?

Was I suddenly in a hallway? Had I taken a wrong turn in my sleep? What if I got stuck here and couldn't get around the wall? After what seemed like ages, but could have been mere seconds, minutes or hours, I decided to see if I could push the wall, back down into its rightful place. To my surprise and joy – it worked – the illusory wall fell forward and re-joined the road surface and onward we moved.

The second incident was food related. At some point I had a moment of clarity and realised I had been in the middle of the road (which still functioned as a truck route) attempting to pick up a bowl of granola. Not only did I really want the bowl (I'm a big fan of granola) but I was getting inordinately frustrated as my gloved fingers slipped through the ethereal bowl – leaving it intact on the road and me empty handed. The moment of clarity revealed the folly of my quest. I stood, shook my head and moved on.

At some point in the early hours, I caught sight of Tim, which buoyed my spirits. He must have slowed down as well for me to catch him with my vastly reduced pace. Maybe the first three-hour block had given me more of a catch up on the field than I thought. I tried to pick up the pace but he seemed elusive again, in fact no matter what I did I couldn't seem to close the gap, in fact he eventually seemed to be drawing away from me. My frustration was heart breaking, in tears I started 'running' in a desperate bid to reach him. It seemed to make no difference, as I would come over a rise I would be greeted by the vista of another long, undulating stretch of road, devoid of human life.

My back was now screaming at me. In a bid to circumvent the loading, I stopped and dragged out my homemade chest harness – my plan B – that would allow me to distribute the load not only to my hips but also over my shoulders. The thinking being that the shoulder harness would help pull me into a more upright posture and give me a chance at holding a better, and less painful, position. As my frozen fingers fiddled and fought with clasps and buckles, the remaining competitor behind me, Hidechika, closed in and passed me. Tears rolled down my cheeks, I swore at all and sundry within earshot (which only meant that the road and the trees and my sled copped a verbal barrage worthy of Samuel L Jackson) until finally I was on my way again. Literally within a kilometre it became clear that my harness solution was in fact no solution at all – it only made matters worse. Another stop, more precious time spent getting frozen fingers and hands as I packed it away and re-rigged the original aluminium poles and waist harness. The sun rose and I looked up to the sky, knowing that the time for admitting some uncomfortable truths was nigh.

It's an interesting process, talking about this expedition publicly as I regularly do and being granted the ability to verbally, and mentally, deconstruct what was, at the time, such a raw and gut-wrenching few hours. What I tell people is that life isn't a Hollywood movie – and no matter how much I willed it or wanted it, the Bill Conti theme from Rocky was not going to suddenly rise up in the background to help me overcome. There would be no last minute revelation or discovery or saviour that would turn the tide of my fortunes and see me stride into Tsig ready to tackle the second half of the race as an entirely new athlete. You do not rise to the occasion; you fall to the level of your training. My training was found to be lacking. My plan was lacking. My execution of the plan was poor. My ability to adapt and adjust had been found to be insufficient.

I stopped and took stock. Both my ankles had locked up, vastly reducing their degree of movement. My back was on strike and looking to leave for better employment. I was tragically slow, hallucinating and literally starving. I had dropped approximately a kilogram in bodyweight every 24 hours. The next section of the race would see us depart the Dempster Highway and move onto the Peel River – frozen, open, exposed and the beginning of two of the longest and most remote sections of the entire race. These sections would make the previous days look relatively warm and comfortable in comparison. I looked to the sky and asked both my son, Campbell, and wife, Ilona to forgive me. It was over. The next checkpoint would see me tap out. I wiped the tears off my face, stood and headed into what I thought would be the last few kilometres into Tsig.

Turns out they would be more than just a few kilometres. Tsig in spring is a beautiful place, but in winter it is frozen and locked away – I could see the town and understood where I needed to go but literally could not see any way to get there. The road swept around to my left and then headed over the river and off towards the next checkpoint. Tsig was on my right but was separated from me by a huge escarpment. I walked for two hours trying to locate the road into town, gradually getting more frustrated and feeling more defeated. What I didn't know was that to access the town we had to literally go past it, swing onto the frozen Peel River – where Murray was waiting in his black Suburban to walk us in. Finally I spotted him, Hidechika was with him and he told us to follow his vehicle and he would lead us into the town and to the checkpoint.

That walk was long. When you are so close to a checkpoint,

especially one where you knew your journey would end, every kilometre seemed endless. Finally, after meandering through endless tracks, streets and seemingly never-ending short steep hills, we reached the checkpoint – a small community centre.

When I walked inside I must have looked like the walking dead – I stumbled into the bathroom and caught sight of myself in the mirror. I looked like someone had put me through a sandblasting machine. Aged and exhausted, I had definitely had better days. No Instagram filter was undoing that level of degradation. When I came out into the main area I was greeted by a few surprises. Neil K – an athlete I hadn't seen since the Arctic Circle CP was here and officially scratched. I had him pegged as being not only a certain finisher but most likely a podium finisher. His departure from the field, while a shock, was actually of some comfort. In some way it seemed to validate my choice – if an athlete of his calibre was not finishing then my exit seemed entirely justified. Tim was in the common room, trying to get his mobile phone to work – he looked up at me and told me, 'It's over, I'm out, I can't do it'. My response was simple, 'Thank God, so am I.'

I turned to Hully, one of the support crew and tapped on the table, tap, tap – 'I'm out'.

His answer was typically Australian, 'Bullshit, you're fine, grab a snooze and some food and let's get back to work.'

'I'm done mate, it's over. I've done the math; I know my body. If I keep going you'll be picking me up off the side of the road tomorrow, a frozen human being.'

'Then I'll drive by and pick you up mate, that's what I'm here for, so sleep, eat and give it a crack, I'll come and get you if you need me.'

Hully is an epic human, a great Aussie and while I appreciated his urging me on, I knew it was over. Martin came over to check in and see if he could talk me out of it. Sorry mate. Decision made.

I stepped outside and rang my wife with tears in my eyes. I'm sorry, I can't do it. She asked if I had another step left in me. I didn't. Then you're done, it's ok, come home. I rang my Mum as well to let her know I was safe but done and dusted. I unrolled my swag, ate some food and collapsed into my sleeping bag. As I took off my shoes, I could see the swelling around my feet, ankles and the weird cramped up balls of muscle, fascia and tissue that dotted their way up my shins. Those legs were done. At some point, I think it was about three to four hours later, Hully woke me up.

'Mate, Pete and Tim have decided to head out together and keep going. I have to ask – do you want to join them? This is it.'

'No. I can't, thanks mate, I'm done.'

The news that Tim was heading back out took me by surprise, he had seemed adamant that he was done, but by the same token, if he was going to continue on, then going with Pete was a sound choice. A great bloke, calm, solid and seemingly invincible, just grinding out the kilometres with little concern for being fast or racing, just getting the job done. Talking with Tim after the race, especially back home, he seemed remorseful that he had told me he was out and then changed his mind. As if in some way he had deceived me and influenced my decision to quit. Nothing could be further from the truth – I was done no matter what he did. If it hadn't been for his companionship and support way back at James Creek I still wonder if I would have made it past CP2, some 150km further back from where we were now.

The next few days were a blur – you are suddenly just a default part of the crew, thrown in with the gear and sleds of everyone else and travelling along the road as the remaining athletes continued their slow grind to Tuk. Two days later we would come across Pete and Tim, sitting down on the Peel River trying to get their stove working to make 'a brew' as Pete is so fond of calling it. The fiddling around while trying to warm his fuel enough to actually light the stove, combined with spilling some water on his hands would leave Pete with frostbitten fingers, blistered and swollen for weeks. As we pulled up beside them they announced that they too were done. Simple maths, they couldn't move fast enough to get to the finish in time – even though the finish was literally days away. They too knew that their time to admit that the race was over had arrived. Their withdrawal would take the number of remaining athletes to six – out of the starting 23 – and those six would all make it to the end.

Finally we reached the shores of the frozen Arctic Ocean and the snow-covered Inuit township of Tuktoyaktuk. We set up base in the gymnasium of the local school – the sleeping mats and gear of race crew, support crew and withdrawn athletes scattered around the basketball court. From here we waited out the final days and hours as the remaining athletes staggered in. I would come out to see each and every one of them finish – happy for them, secretly shattered for my own performance. I should clarify that while gutted to not finish, I knew that I had done everything in my power to get as far as possible. I didn't feel like I had let myself down or quit early or folded and just decided it was 'all too hard'. I had thrown everything but the kitchen sink out of my arsenal at this race and had simply found my toolkit to be lacking. It was the right decision, but that didn't make the reality any less painful.

The final athlete to cross the line was Scott D – someone who has not only become a great friend but would become an invaluable resource in my preparation for 2019. He crossed the line, managed to grab an hour or so of rest before being bundled into the cars with everyone else for the long drive back to Eagle Plains and eventually to Whitehorse. From a physiological perspective I can't imagine how painful it must have been to be so physically beaten after the best part of eight days of racing only to be squeezed into a car for two long days of ceaseless driving – not the ideal recovery scenario.

Suddenly we're back in Whitehorse – civilisation. The pain and sleep deprivation and sheer magnitude of the wilderness that I should have traversed started to fade a little. On the last night before the departures began for people to head back to the 'real world' and their 'normal lives' there was an award ceremony. Everyone got a trophy. Everyone. Didn't matter if you finished the entire distance or pulled out five kilometres off the start line – we all got a small Inukshuk. The podium finishers got slightly larger ones with the winner, the Romanian Tibi, getting the winner's trophy. Despite being listed by Red Bull and Outside Magazine as one of the toughest races in the world, there is no prize money, and no one is there for that anyway. We were all there for the experience, the adventure, the magnitude of the challenge and the majesty of the Arctic.

When my name was called, I walked up, shook Martin's hand and took my little trophy. I muttered something under my breath that came out unexpectedly for me, I'm not even sure if Martin heard it – but we will come back to what I said later.

The trophy seemed so incongruous to me, my effort, while being the best I had, didn't seem to warrant a trophy. I hadn't finished. Hell I hadn't seen half the course. I knew all the platitudes of getting there is an achievement in itself, you outlasted the vast majority of the field, you managed an incredible distance in tough conditions. I know, I know. But it just didn't sit right. I was not OK with this. Another day in Whitehorse and then the long thirty-hour haul back almost 14,000km to home.

I arrived, jet lagged, exhausted and somewhat stunned. I brought home an amazing story, incredible images, experiences and friendships that will last a lifetime. But something else had come home with me. It took up no space in my baggage yet weighed heavy upon me. It would be ever present, most often quietly but always in the background. It would cast a shadow and pose questions. Its very existence could be a destructive force or a guiding light.

That choice would be mine.

There were decisions to be made.

CHAPTER 8

The decision

Warrnambool, Victoria, Australia
March 2018

FRIENDS AND FAMILY WILL OFTEN SAY to me that from their perspective my decision to return to the Arctic was nothing more than a forgone conclusion and that the last person to realise it was me. Deep down I believe that there is some fundamental truth to that – but perhaps for me it was slightly more complicated. From the outside it seems like a fairly black and white choice – am I going back or not? But for me either answer came with its own mountain of baggage and realities to deal with.

If I decide to call it quits, there is the comfort of knowing that it is over. The training is over – no more ridiculously early mornings and crazy overnight runs. No more agonising over spreadsheets, planning pacing, strategising nutrition. No more sacrifices from family and friends when the hours of prep mount up and the time comes once more to leave home. I can stop – I have nothing to prove. I went and gave it absolutely everything I had and slogged it out far into the wilderness. I can close that book.

But that's the problem isn't it? The book will be closed – and can I live with that? Forever?

On his return from his 2019/2020 epic winter Arctic Circle crossing (including almost 1300km on skis dragging sleds weighing between 160 and 180kg each), the adventurer Mike Horn said that while he and fellow adventurer Borge Ousland were out in the never-ending darkness, fighting for every kilometre, running out of supplies, running out of time and facing seemingly insurmountable odds at every turn, out there is where he felt most alive. But, he noted, while out there, he was doing everything he could to make it back 'here' – to civilisation and the real world, his comfort zone – the place where he felt the least alive. He simply shook his head noting how strange we adventuring humans are.

I understand his perspective but feel there is a crucial point missing. We throw ourselves into the greatest of adventures to feel alive, only to strive to return to a place where we feel ourselves as being 'less'. It's as if that self-imposed hardship, that painful stripping away of all that is civilised, casts us into stark and immolating light. A light so incandescent that it shreds even shadows – leaving only our original self, garbed in nothing but our own will and ferocity. A savage who, while lost in the towers of the civilised world, recognises his home amongst the raw and indefatigable onslaught of Mother Nature.

The point of all of this I believe is not to feel that the 'non-adventuring you' is somehow less alive, but to learn how to take that light, that savage ferocity and harness it, to bring it back with you from the edges of the world, back to 'civilisation' and to let it light you for all the days ahead. Go out and have your adventure but let it fill you to the brim so that when you return all your days are alive, so that those around you – family, friends – get the most alive version of you. For they have often sacrificed too – maybe not in sweat and toil, but in their own way – so that you may go to the edges and fill your void.

Back to that decision – can I live with the book being closed? I was satisfied that I had given everything I had in that race, that there was no chance of me making the finish let alone the next checkpoint. But – the experience had changed me. I returned a different person – what I had gained was knowledge and perspective. I had seen the enormity of the task in all its naked beauty. And it was beautiful. I knew what could go wrong, how it could go wrong and most importantly, I had a new-found reserve of knowledge on what could be done differently. I looked at that book and noted the bookmark still buried well within a chapter. There was more to this tale.

I remember the discussion very clearly. Actually, I remember both times I had this discussion with Ilona about the 6633. The first time in 2016 I had brought it up over coffee and breakfast at our favourite Sunday morning haunt, 'How would you feel about me tackling an ultra-marathon in Canada, would probably mean two-to-three weeks away?' After almost a decade together Ilona knew that this wasn't a flippant question, a spur of the moment decision – she knew me well enough to know that this would have been rolling around in my cranium for some time before being brought before the powers that be for a green light. A few key questions – details, safety, risk, logistics and a swift decision of support – she is nothing if not decisive, my wife. The second time we had that conversation, in 2018, I have no doubt that she knew it was coming. Sitting on the couch one night:

'So, just thinking, if I wanted to, you know we would need to look at…'

She cut me off mid-sentence.

'When did registrations open?'

'Oh I'm not entirely sure, maybe a five or six minutes ago'

'Go sign up. We'll figure it out'

Nothing happens without her, but everything that does happen is because of her.

I sat on it for the night, just rolling it around in my mind. Not whether I would go back, that decision had been well and truly made, I just wanted those last few moments before I paid my money and it all became very, very real. I was under no illusions; I knew what it meant. A few minutes on the internet, the electronic flight of some of my hard-earned cash and all of a sudden the cascade of realities would come forth. The training, the preparation, the doubt, the excitement, the risk, the questions, all of it would come forth and be unavoidable. When all this was over, the questions would have been answered and the final chapter of the book would well and truly have been written – regardless of the outcome.

In some sense my return was inevitable but armed now with the knowledge of what a decision like that meant resulted in some soul searching and 'hard conversations' – all with myself.

There won't be a third chance, you're lucky enough to be getting a second one. It can't be wasted, you can't be flippant, or frivolous or dishonest with yourself. If we are doing this then we are going all the way, and that comes with some realities – and not only for you. We'd grown from a family of three to a family of four. Not only would my time away racing leave my wife with two young boys as well as an almost full-time job to juggle, but even the training would ask for significant sacrifice from them – sure you can train at night or odd hours so you don't cut your time with the boys, or shirk your responsibilities at home, but someone is still left home alone while you are out doing the work. It would take more than just great time management, it would be an effort from everyone to get done what had to be done.

The next day, I filled out the application form, ticked the 'returning athlete' box and sent my money. A little time later I got a message from Martin – 'I'm so excited that you're coming back, you'll love the new course, it's flippin' brilliant.' Oh yeah, had I mentioned the course had changed from 2017? Due to access route changes, the course now involved a much longer river section and the final 'stretch' from Inuvik to Tuk would be on the new access road. All in all that meant we were in for a longer race – from 583km in 2017 to 614km in 2019. Greater distance came with a greater time cap at least – the race would start at 10:30am on the Thursday and athletes would have until 10:30am on Saturday of the following week to be over the line or out. Allowing for a time change as we moved from the Yukon into the Northwest Territories as well as switch to daylight savings time, meant that all up we would have 216 hours to get the distance done.

It sounds like an enormous amount of time – but that clock was relentlessly, tireless, unstoppable, every hour, every day, without remorse. In the silence of the Arctic wilderness the ticking of that clock could become very loud indeed.

So now it is April 2019.

'Alea iacta est' – the die is cast, so muttered Caesar as he crossed the Rubicon.

What happens next?

We do what needs to be done.

No quarter.

Time to do the work.

CHAPTER 9

Do. The. Work.

Warrnambool, Victoria, Australia
April 2017 – March 2018

THERE IS VALUE IN THE NAIVETY that comes with tackling a race for the first time – but it's a double edged sword. You have the comfort of not necessarily knowing what is coming around the next corner, or over the next hill, so while there is uncertainty, there usually isn't dread. You just head out and deal with whatever comes. The flip is that you don't know what's coming so all you can do is head out and deal with whatever comes – and find out on the fly whether you were adequately prepared…or not.

> 'The electric light did not come from the continuous improvement of candles…'
> *Oren Harari*

This time we started with a clean training slate. My 2017 training had seen me well prepared for what I had expected, not what I encountered. This time I made a commitment to develop a broad and deep toolkit that would leave me ready to face all and sundry that the race, the Arctic and my own inner dialogue/demons could throw at me.

First step was to enjoy a big piece of humble pie and accept that maybe, just maybe, I don't know as much about endurance training as I thought I did. I'm fairly well versed but something of this magnitude would not tolerate 'pretty good'. It would demand excellence and even then, may still unceremoniously cast me aside.

Step 1 – find the smartest people in the room when it comes to endurance training.

Step 2 – do everything they say, no matter whether I think it's 'right' or 'working'.

I had pretty much a full year to train and prep so we would play the long game. There was plenty of time for adaptation, refinement, testing, resting and everything in between. We would start with the basics and build an entirely new athlete, from the ground up. Keeping in mind that I would hit the start line in 2019 at 43 years of age. Much as I joked about it, the reality was my body didn't bounce back like you do in your twenties; we would need to be smart about recovery, volume, mechanics, nutrition – you know, all that stuff that people want to gloss over because it doesn't look great on Instagram.

The smartest people in the room weren't hard to find, in fact I had worked with them many years before. I had come across CrossFit Endurance in my early development as a CrossFit Trainer, meeting Jason Donaldson at CrossFit Geelong on a training seminar. The brains behind that course, Brian Mackenzie, had, over the coming years, morphed those fundamentals into what would become 'SHIFT//ADAPT'. To me, this was the thinking man's coaching template – it was heavy on the science, heavy on technique and was rigorously tested, by the athletes and coaches themselves. I should clarify, I'm not sponsored or remunerated by them in any way – I signed up to their training program like anyone else. Downloaded the app and began my journey of training.

To give you a quick lay of the land on how they approached the training – a training 'block' was nine weeks in length, comprised of 'test, build, build, build, deload, build, build, test, recovery' – a week dedicated to each. The focus was not on relentless kilometres for the sake of it – but refining technique and capacity. First, learn how to run one kilometre beautifully, making sure you have developed an aerobic capacity to match. Then you can run beautiful kilometre after kilometre – unbroken, un-injured, efficient, relaxed and strong. Just the way nature intended it.

So I put aside any notions I had of my own knowledge and did what I was told. Cadence drills, positioning drills, interval work, mobility. On top of that, I worked on my aerobic efficiency, which meant closing my mouth and breathing through my nose to develop CO_2 (carbon dioxide) tolerance to increase my O_2 (oxygen) efficiency. (The scientist in me revelled in the biochemistry.) This required the need to develop a calm state of mind, especially in the early days of training, as my mind wanted to panic and demand I blow off that CO_2 and suck in some more air, despite the lack of **urgent physiological** need to do so. It's a deep rabbit hole if you want to descend it, well beyond the scope of why we are here now.

The other reason I loved their training was the time – when you don't have to find a way to jam these epically long runs into your training you suddenly have more time available. To begin with I was training once a day every day – a far cry from my twice a day regimen previously. Generally I was done and dusted in an hour. If you don't mess about, finding an hour isn't that impossible, particularly if you're happy to move that hour into the dark side of the day. Early mornings, late nights, they are hours just the same as any other. As the months crept by, I knew the long work would come, I would have to work it in but to begin with it was all mechanics and base building.

For me in those early days, the hardest part was simply trusting the process. This was vastly different to what I had done previously, not necessarily the components – the work itself was nothing new – but how it was constructed, the amount, the prescribed intensity. Having faith in the process was a bit of a paradigm shift.

'...We burn a hot fire here; it melts down all concealment...'
Arthur Miller, The Crucible

I logged everything. Every training session, load, reps, times, distances, rest days – planned or otherwise. All of it. Partly to maintain the discipline of doing the work and partly as a brutally honest assessment of how I was travelling. What were the times doing – the loads, heart rate, recovery? Each nine-week block was set out in a printed calendar – old school, I actually wrote everything down. Alongside the training, I would set other 6633 specific goals for each block. Usually this was a race I had entered, some race-specific additional training I wanted to complete (especially as the months rolled on) and usually some logistics work. So for example, in my third block of training I wanted to add some regular tyre drags, a long sled pull (25–40km), complete a specific trail race (50km+) and finalise any kit purchases of race gear. This helped keep me focused and stay on track – rather than trying to add in a ridiculous amount of volume in the last few months before March 2019, I was gradually building, giving myself time to refine, reflect and recover. This process also helped keep the concept of playing the long game top of mind – as the kilometres started to accumulate and the sled pulls and tyre drags got longer, there was a gradual evolution both physically and mentally, which allowed me to settle in and find a rhythm, adjustments in pace, equipment, loading and mental dialogue. This all focused around the need to be able to execute extreme long distances without deterioration in physical structure or mental stamina. Those long hours had to become a place to be comfortable and content within – no matter what the outside world was hurling at me.

So what did a 'normal' week of training look like? For starters the concept of 'normal' was an evolving concept – what I considered 'normal' in Block 1 in April 2018 compared to my final block, Block 6 in Jan 2019 was markedly different. Having said that, the global tenets remained. The original training concept around how the week was broken down was as follows:

Monday – Strength and conditioning with main focus on strength. Usually a fundamental lift – squat, deadlift, cleans. Finish with some short conditioning piece, usually 10–12 minutes

Tuesday – Run, short interval repeats (anywhere from 100m–400m distances).

Wednesday – Strength and conditioning, usually more an upper body focus with a similar short time-frame conditioning piece.

Thursday – Run, long interval repeats (400m–1000m distances).

Friday – Strength and conditioning, a little more event/sport specific compared to the more fundamental lifts.

Saturday – Long distance – sled, run or ruck.

Sunday – Active recovery.

So in short – six days of serious work and a day of active recovery. For me, active recovery started out as long walks, then evolved to slow bike work. As the training load increased and the volume stepped up, the active recovery become even more important and would typically involve sauna, contrast therapy (hot and cold alternating baths) and plenty of yoga/mobility work. At 43 years of age, being 'supple' was not exactly a natural state of being for me, so there was always plenty of work to do to unglue muscles and fascia and restore some range of motion to joints that had accumulated no small volume of kilometres.

Throughout those last few months before hitting the start line, the heavier work dropped off and the long work became more the focus. February tapered off towards the end of the month with travel and preparation.

Integrated with those long sessions was training and testing gear, processes, strategies. The old runner's adage of 'nothing new on race day' still held – the last thing I needed was to discover a few hours into a potentially 200+ hour race that my harness rubbed on a particular spot or a piece of equipment I thought was magnificent was rendered useless in -30C either because of temperature or because wearing multiple gloves and/or mitts made it impossible to manipulate.

Probably one of the best examples of this equipment/strategy testing I can give is how I approached food prep and consumption for race conditions. Having a total time cap of over 200 hours sounds like an almost indulgent amount of time – but I know from bitter experience, even in long races at home, that that clock was relentless and ticked away regardless of whether you were busy making distance on the trail or sitting on your posterior at a checkpoint feeling sorry for yourself. Time marches on. I wanted to ensure that not only was I shovelling enough calories into the 'furnace' but that I wasn't wasting any time doing it. To that end, I devised a system and method of preparing freeze-dried meals on the move – I could prepare the meal, eat it, wash out my wide mouth thermos and reload it with the next meal and not need to break stride. Now that may seem like a little bit of overkill to some – surely you could take the few minutes rest to eat and then get back on the move? You could – but you had to recognise that such an 'indulgent' strategy carries two associated costs. First, as soon as you stop you are getting colder – you are no longer generating heat through movement – and trust me, it is really noticeable. Within roughly thirty seconds of stopping you can feel that cold seeping in through your clothes. So now you're not just stopping to get food out, you also have to first get some extra layers on – and then the reverse when you are ready to head off again. The second cost is obviously time – but how much? I worked on the following theory – I estimated a 'meal break' would take approximately ten minutes from start to finish. I also knew that I wanted to eat something of substance (so not just a snack) roughly every four hours. That's six meals a day. That's an hour lost per day. Every day. For potentially eight days. Now you're not talking about ten minutes in isolation anymore – you are talking about eight hours, that could be eight hours of sleep you have bought yourself, or it could be the difference between finishing under the time cap or outside of it (which renders you a DNF – no mercy here). Eight hours to use as necessary – it was simply too great a gift to squander. So on those long training days, power walking the trails with my sled in tow, I refined the process so when I was marching along the Dempster with gloves on, ski goggles on, thermos in hand, I could efficiently 'enjoy' refuelling while still making distance.

Be ruthlessly efficient in all things – no matter how small.

Be intentionally disciplined in all things – no matter how small.

For me, one of the toughest phases of the entire year of training was managing the final few weeks. I felt like I had spent all this time building a robust and capable engine but needed to find that delicate balance of not 'over-cooking' it in those final weeks, while also not dropping off and peaking too early. I knew I would still have a week of travel and prep in Canada before the starter gun. In the end I simply listened to my body – when I felt good I would go and drag the tyre or hit the bike. If I felt a little weary then I rested, hit the sauna, did yoga or mobility work. Packed and unpacked and repacked the sled – usually with the 'help' of our two young boys.

This was not the time to try and set a personal best in heavy lifts or gun for a time trial record. Maintain the body, clear the mind, give the body a chance to loosen and settle – so when the time came to drive it to oblivion it would be ready. I think it was Rich Froning Jnr who said, 'in training you listen to your body, but in competition you tell your body to shut up…'

It was about time to take this shiny 'new' chassis to the start line and see what it could do.

CHAPTER 10

Ladies and gentlemen – it's time

I LEANT FORWARD IN MY Air Canada seat and looked at the window seat on the opposite side of the aisle – the 'seat' I had booked for my flight home in a little over three weeks' time. When I came to sit in that seat – the questions would all have been answered. The race would be over and I would know. Did I make it to Tuk, how had the race unfolded, what had the weather done, would I have bandaged fingers from frostbite or a warmth from the knowledge of a job well done? That 'future me' would be sitting in that seat and know it all – would he look back over at this seat and smile or just shake his head and sink dejectedly back into his seat.

The journey was almost a mirror image of the one I had taken in 2017 – same thirty-odd hours of flights and layover, same sequence of flights and times, I had simply moved it a few days earlier to give myself an extra 48 hours in Whitehorse to prep and throw off any jet lag before I began forcibly denying my body any semblance of rest or sleep. This journey perhaps lacked some of the naive excitement about the journey to come but it did come with a sense of greater calm. There was comfort in knowing the flights, the layovers, the processes that would take me 14,000km from my home on the coast of the Southern Ocean, all the way to begin my journey to the Arctic Ocean.

After that final short flight from Vancouver to Whitehorse, I wandered up to the very basic baggage carousel and arrivals lounge at Whitehorse Airport and began the nervous wait to see if my luggage actually managed to make the entire journey with me. Race director Martin and support crew member/race photographer Evan were there to meet incoming athletes for the flight and to transport us into town and the Coast High Country Inn, home and staging point for the competitors. My oversized bags holding my sled and all manner of survival gear had indeed made it, and along with another returning athlete, Kurt, we made our way into Whitehorse.

Once settled in at the High Country, I dumped my bags in my room and immediately headed out. It was lunchtime here and my standard operating procedure whenever I have made a long haul flight anywhere is to get out for a long walk in the daylight as soon as possible. In this case I also had the additional purpose of hitting up some speciality suppliers to start collating my food and supplies. The brisk air of Whitehorse, hovering around a relatively warm -5_C to -10_C was the perfect slap in the face after such a long time trapped in flying metal tubes surrounded by stale recycled air. The shopping list was fairly extensive – mainly just in terms of sheer volume of food. I couldn't bring much with me both due to weight restrictions – my sled and gear had maxed out any load allowance that came with my ticket – and the customs regulations also prevented me from hauling in much in the way of particular preferred food items. As I stood in the freeze-dried and snack section of Coast Mountain Sports, selecting freeze-dried meals based not on culinary preference but purely on the amount of calories per meal (turns out granola and desserts where big hitters in that department, surprise, surprise) a staff member wandered past eying the growing pile in my basket, 'You know you can't return any food items once they have left the store?' Yep, all good, I'm hoping to devour every single one of these. A few hours and two trips to offload bags of food, stove fuel and snacks later and the afternoon was done.

Dinner at High Country was a tradition, as more and more athletes arrived – some new faces and some friends from 2017. More often than not, the majority of the field comprises returning athletes – another stark reminder that this race takes no prisoners and lets few pass unscathed all the way to Tuk.

All in all, over the next two days I would begin new friendships and refresh past ones. On the returning side of the ledger were athletes such as fellow Australian Matt Size, a man with a permanent wide grin and true laconic style, and Neil Kapoor from the UK, who had sported a very serious black beard in 2017, but turned up here fresh faced but, like me, very aware of what lay before us. Neil had a serious racing pedigree and I had actually expected him to podium in 2017. A range of factors, not the least of which may have been a close call one night with unexpected road traffic on the way to Tsiigetchic, had led to him pulling out – but he was back like so many of us. Also returning from 2017 was David

Smale, a true veteran on the 6633, David was returning for attempt number six, bringing with him a prodigious knowledge of the Arctic, the terrain ahead of us and its history. Bronwyn Hull was also a returnee from 2017. Her husband Michael (aka 'Hully') had successfully completed the 580km distance a few years prior and as I previously regaled, had crewed the race in 2017. On the crew side, both the medics from 2017, Jonny and Scotty, were back and it felt like having them both there would give me an opportunity to redeem my earlier performance and close the circle so to speak. Both men are incredibly knowledgeable and diligent in their tasks; they would become lifelines for us all in the tough days ahead.

The next 48 hours – Sunday and Monday – were a strange mix of preparation and trying to get as much rest as possible, while simultaneously managing the growing sense of the impending race. All that training, the relentless hours and days spent crafting an engine and psyche that was now bubbling and chafing, just itching to be set loose to do its great and terrible work. You're simultaneously trying to keep a lid on it while not letting the flames get too low. My solution was to focus on the steps – the incremental work that needed to be done. Buying all the food was one step, prepping it was another – and the scientist in me had been looking forward to (and working on) this for some time. I had learnt the hard way in 2017 that all the best laid plans are great, those coloured excel spreadsheets look amazing at home, but if they are functionally impractical then all the planning in the world isn't going to save your frozen, starving, shambling frame in the endless tundra.

Food prep and plan went as follows. Goal was 6400 calories per 24 hours. Allowing for the fact that I would probably under eat, if I came in close to 6000 that was acceptable, if I happened to get the full amount then yay for me. Those calories would come from a mix of full freeze-dried meals, 'mini meals', 'hots' and my carefully-constructed trail mix snack packs.

The full freeze-dried meals were usually 800–1200 calories per meal – any packaging claims of 'contains two servings' were summarily ignored. Everything, regardless of size, was now single serve. 'Mini-meals' were generally freeze-dried with a lower caloric punch in the 600–800 range. They were smaller and less dense so easier to consume and digest on the move. The 'hots' were soups, noodles, hot chocolate, recovery drinks – fast to prepare, easy to consume, providing the double win of giving warmth both physiologically and psychologically. The snack bags were 1000-calorie bags of trail mix – all crafted in the comfort of my hotel room at Whitehorse. These were going to be my go-to snack, stored in a wide-mouth Nalgene bottle attached to my hip or sled for easy access – they would be the ongoing top up of calories. I bought the basic ingredients – biscuits, power bars, energy bars, chocolate, chia seeds, nuts, ginger cookies and so forth, then calculated the number of calories per item – as in per cookie, per Smartie, per piece of power bar (I cut every bar into eight bite-size portions with my trusty pocketknife). Using that knowledge, I divided the mix into piles. Each pile consisted of the following: one-and-a-quarter power bars, three pieces of Peak caffeinated dark chocolate, three ginger biscuits (crushed), 100g trail mix, 40g Smarties, 20g Hersheys mix, 15g cacao nibs.

Put it all in a ziplock bag and boom – 1000 calories per bag. Pour the bag into the hard plastic Nalgene bottle, shake and tip into mouth as required. When the bottle was empty I'd know I'd downed 1000 calories. Pour another bag in to reload – a stunningly simply and effective system.

So for much of those two days, my hotel room looked more like the disarrayed storeroom at a supermarket and camping food store than anything else. I needed over 30 freeze-dried meals, two dozen 'hots', at least a dozen of my trail mix snack bags and then, most importantly, some drop bag treats – those special items you could dream about on the trail knowing that when you get to the drop bag checkpoints – Fort Mac and Inuvik – there would be something amazing waiting for you. In my case I had these ridiculous family size gourmet flavoured Kit Kats waiting for me – espresso and dark chocolate ganache flavoured, the real deal. I was more excited by them than the fresh pair of socks.

Lastly was the water requirements that come with such a nutrition plan – you plan on eating that many freeze-dried and that's a fair amount of water – that you have to carry – to make it all happen. Based on my calculations I would need approximately 4000ml of water per 24 hours, just to prep the food. Work backwards from there, how long between checkpoints, allow for some delay or emergency and then load up accordingly. My final system was three main thermoses – 2L and two 1.2L plus a 700ml for hot drinks. In addition, I had a race vest on under my clothes that had a CamelBak system – at checkpoints I would fill this with 1.5–2L of very hot water.

This would serve two purposes: initially it would keep me warm and secondly it would give me ready access to water for the sole purpose of staying hydrated versus preparing food.

Once everything was sorted, chopped, packed and divided up, the last step was to set it out per day and therefore see what could go into drop bags for further down the trail and what needed to be packed on the sled ready to roll right from day one. That allowed me to pack my drop bags as per race regulations – they had to be small and relatively light. You couldn't have a full resupply of everything at the checkpoints, you had two bags for the entire 614km and they had to be the bare essentials.

Lastly, that meant the sled could be packed, and unpacked, and repacked, and unpacked and finally repacked for the last time. Once they were loaded onto the truck at Whitehorse we would not see them until the night before the race at Eagle Plains, with limited time for any last-minute adjustments and no access to any additional supplies. If you didn't have it now then you'd better figure out a way to survive without it.

One of the traditions of the pre-race days in Whitehorse is the 'test-drive' – mandatory for first timers and recommended for returnees – it entailed an afternoon sortie with loaded sled for a few miles of trail with a break during which athletes had to establish their bivvy, light their stove and produce a cup of tea. Sounds fairly innocuous but for the race crew it was establishing that all athletes, in the event of being stuck on the trail, waiting for rescue, would be able to set up shelter and get a hot drink going – garnering them some degree of safety from the elements and a means of warmth and hydration until help arrived.

The test drive started with everyone meeting in a car park near the landmark of the ice-bound USS Klondike paddle steamer.

I remember this particular gathering very clearly, it was really the first opportunity that everyone has to really check out all our fellow athletes with race kit in tow. I had chosen to tag along sans sled as I had been through the process already and was confident in my equipment – but wanted to come along for the walk and to enjoy the camaraderie of old friends and establish some connection with those I didn't know. It was my first look at three racers in particular – Avram, Patrick and Didier. All three men came with prior race experience and performance pedigree. The general consensus seemed to be that those three would be battling it out for the podium in no uncertain terms. All three had attempted the 2018 race – a race that had seen severe and extreme weather over Wrights Pass, wiping out a multitude of racers almost instantly. Patrick had been in a strong second position when he scratched at Aklavik due to frostbite concerns – second to 6633 legend Romanian Tiberiu Useriu (Tibi), a three-time winner and, as of writing, current race record holder for the longer 580km course that had first been run in 2018.

I had come with the clear and sole purpose of simply finishing the race – first, last, middle of the pack, I didn't care. My sole goal was the successful completion of the entire 614km on my own terms and under the time cut-off. I came with the mental attitude that the kilometres were getting done and would pay no mind to my position in 'the pack'. But, if I am completely honest, I had trained with the mindset of 'what would it take to win it?' The mental model behind this was not that I thought I could win, but that if I had trained the capacity to be that good, then no matter what the Arctic chose to throw at me, I would have the reserves required to get the job done. I'd leave the winning part to the real athletes. And while all that is well and good I would be lying if I said I looked at those three men and didn't feel somewhat intimidated and did some quiet nervous questioning of my own potential.

Avram looked every bit the part – his sled bag was literally covered in sponsors' badges and logos, he had brought along a small crew to film and record his race. He came with no small back catalogue of amazing endurance feats already, including swimming the entire length of the Danube without a wetsuit. He was small, rugged and looked like the living embodiment of the term 'pocket rocket'. I remember looking at him and thinking, how is anyone going to beat that guy? The more I got to know Avram two things became very clear – he was always happy and he was simply a pleasure to be around. We crossed paths multiple times on the trail in the days ahead and every encounter with him left me happier for the experience.

Didier looked like your more archetypal ultra racer, slight of build, small of stature – even by my diminutive standards – and also possessed of a quiet calm and capacity. He seemed reserved but had the air of someone comfortable in their own ability and ready to do the work – all in an unassuming and introspective manner.

Lastly there was Patrick – I really only got to meet Patrick later that evening when a few of us returning athletes decided to venture out for dinner. We went for the frosty stroll to possibly the best named bar on the planet, the 'Dirty Northern Bastards'.

We all kicked back some pizza and a few ales as we laughed and chatted, as if we didn't have a care in the world, just a few mates out for a feed at the local, as opposed to men and women who would very soon throw themselves into the abyss. Patrick was tall and lean and had that laconic Irish style, laid back, cheerful but with that quiet undertone of probably being hard as nails. He struck me for no particular reason, more of a conglomerate of assessments – to be a front runner that I would not be seeing for the vast duration of the race.

The afternoon test run passed without incident. Once again, most people did a last-minute dash to Coast Mountain Sports to grab those last few 'essential' bits of kit. That's not a criticism of anyone who did that – I did exactly the same thing two years earlier. Painfully, prior experience does come with some perks – you are less likely to panic and second guess. You already know it's going to suck and that you have 100% definitely forgotten something, so don't worry about it.

The drive to Eagle Plains, which had been a two day drive in 2017, was now a single-day haul of epic proportions – early start in Whitehorse and the long convoy heads off for the 800+km drive. I'm fairly sure that spending over twelve hours cramped up in a car seat the day before the race is probably a move that would send my physiotherapist and chiropractor into complete apoplexy, but it is what it is. Best plan for some time to unfold and stretch out those hip flexors and spine in the hotel room at Eagle Plains – I'll need it. The drive itself was relatively uneventful so I won't burden you with tales of cruising up the Alaskan, Klondike and Dempster highways. Out of respect I will note that we travelled through the lands of the following First Nations; Champagne and Aishihik, Little Salmon, Carmacks, Tr'ondek Hwech'in and Tetlit Gwich'in.

There was one meeting at Eagle Plains that requires mentioning – it was here that we would catch up with Pete Newland. Pete is one of the more fascinating individuals I have ever had the chance to meet – we both attempted the race in 2017 and Pete had been the last person to pull out. He had returned in 2018 and successfully completed the distance and was now riding a fat bike, solo and unassisted from Whitehorse all the way to Tuk – a journey of some 1500km. Pete uses his adventures to raise funds for an organisation called 'For Rangers' – a company he is co-founder of. They raise funds and then subsequently train and support front line park rangers who continually risk their own welfare and lives protecting endangered species from hunters and poachers. I highly recommend you check them out – they run some amazing events and do incredible work. Pete and I had kept in contact since 2017 and I had been looking forward to seeing him again. Unbeknown to both of us at the time but eight days later he and I would have a brief conversation on the ice road on the way into Tuk and he would give me some advice that I will remember for a very long time.

A big feed and a few beers in the dining room – no need to worry about those 'few extra calories' pretty sure they will be obliterated in no uncertain terms in the coming days – were followed by an early night to try to get some sleep. The race would not start until 10:30 the next morning so there was no hurry – both a blessing and a curse – more time to think and second guess.

After a reasonable night's sleep, all things considered, I tucked into as much breakfast as I dared – I knew I needed it but also didn't want to step up to the start line feeling bloated and overloaded. I grabbed a sugary scroll to stuff into a pocket for later in the morning on the trail, dragged my sled out with everyone else's and proceeded to rest up on the couch in reception. Athletes zipped about here and there – returning athletes generally camped out just waiting, the first timers doing the dance of myriad last minute alterations and adjustments. Watching the first timers flit nervously around I became cognisant of the difference in my own demeanour – compared to the naïve, first timer me two years prior.

Finally the time came. We all lumbered off the couch as if we were off to tend to some menial task, as opposed to the seemingly ridiculous and potentially insurmountable. It was a positively balmy -15C outside with a light snow covering our sleds.

The time had come.

Time to lay all the questions to rest and see what we were made of.

lessons

LESSON 4

Take the hard road

> 'The only true wisdom lives far from mankind, out in the great loneliness, and can be reached only through suffering. Privation and suffering alone opens the mind to all that is hidden to others.'
>
> *Igjugarjuk, Shaman, Caribou Eskimo, Northern Canada*

WHY DO IT? WHY GO THROUGH ALL that training, put yourself through the late nights, the early mornings, the pain, the fatigue, the sacrifice. And to what end? So you can put yourself in a position where you will be tested to your limits, potentially come home empty handed, broken and battered and have what to show for it? As if that wasn't incomprehensible enough, you're doing all of this out of choice – it's not even out of necessity.

And that's the crux of it right there. Choice. For professional athletes, first responders, military, that choice makes sense. But for the rest of us, the 'everyday humans', why choose the hard road?

'…Can you hear the wind Father? Remember what Mother used to say about the wind? The wind cannot defeat the tree with strong roots…'
— *Hawk, 'The Revenant', by Michael Punke*

I bought a copy of Michael Punke's *The Revenant* and after an aborted attempt to get stuck into it, the relatively thin paperback took up silent residence on my bedside table amongst the growing pile of 'to be read'. Almost two years later, for no apparent reason, I decided to give it another go – and I simply couldn't put it down. I devoured the two-hundred-odd pages depicting the true story of frontiersman Hugh Glass in the 1830s American wilderness in a matter of days. I then wrestled our Netflix account out of 'kids' mode so I could track down the film adaptation – regardless of your opinion of the acting (or Tom Hardy's accent) the landscape and cinematography is nothing short of jaw dropping.

But enough of the literary and film review – two themes struck home hard for me – hardship and value.

HARDSHIP

Back to our frontiersmen – they operated in working conditions that would send an occupational health and safety officer into total apoplexy. Months on end, tracking, trapping and trying to prove the viability of a fur trade along the untamed Mississippi. If the bears, wolves, cold exposure or starvation didn't kill you, there's a good chance the indigenous Indian tribes would. That's if you didn't get completely lost in the totally uncharted wilderness, working your way from fort to fort in the desperate hope that when/if you arrive, the fort hasn't been raided, burnt to the ground or just plain abandoned for the winter. These were hard men in every sense of the word. But that very hardship gave them a hauntingly clear metric by which to measure something that many of us today struggle with – a sense of personal value.

Cast a long line back from before the Industrial Age, all the way back to homo sapiens neanderthelensis – either you fought, hunted and provided, stayed healthy and strong or you were out of the tribe. Literally. You were a savage. Not because you chose to be, or thought it was cool or were trying to impress someone – you were a functioning and productive savage because nature demanded it. Between stimulus and response there lies choice (according to Victor Frankel). Sometimes that choice is a conscious one, other times, like our savage forebears, it was driven by our environment and early social construct. You survived and worked together or you died.

'Specific Adaptation though Imposed Demand' – unless you work in the strength and conditioning industry, that's probably not a term you're familiar with. But the reality is, it's not so much a training methodology as it is an undeniable rule of nature. Pressure drives development. Predation, conflict, scarcity of resources, searing heat, bone-cracking cold, drought, flood, fire, plague. You adapted and you survived. Not because it was what you wanted to do but because it was what you had to do.

Stimulus, choice, response – some rules are indefatigable even in the face of evolutionary sized timescales. The rule applies whether it is our savage ancestors fighting for survival or our modern sedentary bodies driving the indentation of our gluteus maximus into the couch, cocooned in a temperature controlled environment, safe from the ravages of weather, marauding hordes, scarcity of food or sabre-tooth tigers. Pressure drives adaptation – and the adaptation will express itself regardless of whether we perceive it to be net positive or negative. For all your deep soul-searching, the reality is you are simply a high-functioning organism that happens to be extremely cognisant of its own existence. Impose the stimulus and the organism will respond and adapt.

Live a 'comfortable' life and your body and your mind will reflect that. The environment for our pre-historic savage was geared towards what I would argue are more positive adaptations – strength, resilience, adaptability – a state of readiness, a recognition of needing to pull your weight.

Now, the modern environment we find ourselves in is also geared towards driving adaptation – just perhaps not the ones we truly need. I would even argue that we have been knowingly and purposely robbed of our capacity for conscious choice and instead had our subconscious quietly caressed and cajoled into making the 'easier' choice. We can have food delivered without getting off the couch, social media apps have entire teams working to ensure that the slavery of psychological addiction keeps us on the screen and out of the sun. As long as it costs more to buy a bottle of water than it does to buy a bottle of soft drink, you can be assured that big business does not have your best interests at heart.

Don't like the cold – stay out of it. Don't like going out, have it delivered. Don't want to deny yourself, then don't. It's the fallacy of believing we are blessed with such a wide array of options when in reality we have been subjugated to comply with the comfortable option. A life that comes with the default 'choice' of comfort is dangerous enough, but now we couple it with both a lack of consequence and a lack of accountability. It's the ultimate triple threat – we are complacently pushed into compliance, we do it because it's easy, there are no obvious consequences and finally, no one is calling us out on it.

It's easy, it doesn't matter and no one cares.

So what? What's the consequence of a life of comfort, gratification and indulgence? So what if I have a #dadbod and I'm happy on the couch eating take out, downing a few beers at night to help me sleep and slamming coffees in the afternoon to keep me awake. If we get unhealthy we see a health professional and take a pill. Heart disease, obesity, type 2 diabetes – this is just the modern condition is it not? That's what the health system is for isn't it? To bail me out at the expense of the taxpayer. Rather than address the behaviour, we simply aim to mask the consequence. It's ok, we have a pill for that. Before the pitchforks and burning torches appear outside my door – yes I realise that not every case of these 'metabolic syndrome' diseases are due to a life of poor choices and indulgence…but a significant number are.

As a pharmacist I have never seen a prescription for exercise, for yoga, meditation, breath-work, for counseling, or one that says, 'Make a better choice – make one per day and call me in two weeks.' Societal safety nets are fundamentally an essential part of a functioning democracy that seeks to lift the standard of living of its citizens. But for many, those safety nets have become hammocks in which we can reside, held aloft by the fallacy of never ending prosperity, the illusion of my unalienable right to comfort and the endemic rewarding of short-termism.

So where are the consequences of the easy life? Normally it comes in the form of accountability – surely someone, somewhere is going to turn up with the big stick. Where has all the accountability gone?

The 'good news' is that the accountability hasn't left. It's been waiting. Biding its time. Assembling. Stalking. And when it does arrive you can rest assured that it will not be a time of your choosing nor in a manner of your liking. I'm not talking about some great biblical judgement – I'm talking about the fundamental laws of nature, of the market, of the human race.

As a father to young boys, I often give this example in workshops – picture yourself at home with family/friends, enjoying a cold beverage on a hot day, ensconced in your favourite outdoor chair and watching the kids zoom around the yard as if energy was an infinite resource to them. An errant kick sends the football down the driveway and out onto the road – your three-year-old decides that this is his time to shine and takes off after it with great gusto and laser-like focus. The driver of the car is, like so many of us, multi-tasking. Tired, situationally unaware, thinking about everything and anything. Your capacity to get out of that chair, to get your body from a dead start to maximum speed and intervene in the nick of time – that capacity and ability is the very manifestation of all those years of 'comfortable choices'. And the bill for those choices is due. Now. If you are unable to pay – your three-year-old will pay the price on your behalf. But it will be paid.

That story doesn't elicit a lot of applause and it certainly doesn't win me any friends. It is usually followed by an uncomfortable silence. Good. Be uncomfortable. Occasionally there might be a brave soul that counters with the argument of, 'You'd rise to the occasion'. Sadly, this isn't an episode of CSI, or Rocky 3. The missing piece of crucial evidence won't appear in the nick of time, Bill Conti's epic theme music won't rise up in the background and suddenly bestow upon you the pace of a leopard and athleticism of a gazelle. Ask any professional athlete – you are only as good as your training. Period. Relying on mystical intervention is simply an excuse. Hope is not a strategy. You're metaphorically kicking the can down the road and saying you'll deal with that when the time comes. Problem is, when the time does come it's more likely to 'arrive' by unexpectedly tearing the front door of your life clean off with all the subtlety of a predator drone strike.

Maybe take a less emotive example – how about just quality of life. Loss of mobility is one of the primary drivers for an ageing population moving out of independent living into assisted care or nursing homes. It's not their mental acuity or metabolic health, they simply can no longer get up off the toilet, or avoid a fall. You were designed to move and move well – ignore that at your peril. Use it or lose it. Watch young children squat, it's a lesson in anatomical proficiency. Great ankle range of motion, neutral spine position, full depth. It looks natural because it is, they can reside in that position ad infinitum and hop straight up and toddle off. Try getting everyone in your office to execute the same squat – and even if they can reach the position, see how long they last. I get that we aren't infants anymore – my femurs are 'marginally' longer now and I've put my hips and ankles through all manner of torture on the trails and in the mountains – but I still actively work to maintain movement and function. Why? Because the alternative is to lose it and suffer the consequences.

Last but not least there is the 'Plan B' imperative – a little more on the darker side but what happens when disaster strikes. Bushfire, flood, the internet goes down for an hour. You may laugh at the last one but a few years ago in my home town, the exchange building for the national telecommunication provider burned down in a freak accident. It knocked out all cellular phone coverage and the internet access for most of the town for almost a week. We may joke about 'what if I can't check 'the socials' or see what my fav insta-celeb is doing?' but this was a lesson in our total dependence. Businesses were suddenly cash only, except that not many people carry enough cash to cover everything for a week, but the ATMs don't work and the banks are struggling as their computer systems don't work either. All of a sudden getting groceries is not as easy as it once was. This was a small fire, in a single building, which inconvenienced a town for a few days. What happens if something far more major occurs. How long can you live out of a backpack for? Sleep on a dirt floor? If the world shifts and petrol is suddenly $10 per litre for six months, can you walk/ride/jog to work?

'Seriously mate, that's not going to happen. We'll know if things are going that far south and I'll get it sorted.' Oh will you? I spent the first few years of my life in the small coastal town of Narooma. As I wrote this book the horrendous wildfires of the Australian summer of 2019/2020 swept along that coast. In the space of 48 hours that town went from modern day normal city to being completely cut off without food, water, power or fuel. No way in and no way out.

You get the point.

Enough of the dark and heavy stuff. I get it, all manner of deprivation and incomprehensible disasters lurk in alleyways and under the floorboards, waiting to pounce. Let's flip the coin for a moment. Let's say I decide to embrace some 'healthy hardship'. Sacrifice some comfort and luxuries. To test the mettle a little, hold the feet to the flames. Is all this just an insurance policy against disaster and decline or does this investment actually deliver in good times as well as bad? Well I'm glad you asked.

We are going to break it down like this.

You have to make a choice.

And to many it will seem like a counter-intuitive choice. Like deciding to swim upstream (works out ok for spawning salmon). Much of the machinations of the modern world will try to drag you back in but you must, as Yeats put it, remain 'captain of your soul'. To truly choose the harder road, because you want it, is a most powerful and liberating act.

You must be disciplined

This is the greatest and most underrated superpower of all. It doesn't require monastic level control, or the sacrificing of all your worldly possessions, you just need to be held accountable by no one other than yourself to do what should be done. Motivational speakers abound – because it is transient. The art of discipline is what burns long after the bunting has been taken down and the refrains of 'Kumbaya' from around the campfire have melted away. I am proof that motivation helps you sign up but discipline puts you on the podium.

You must commit to the long game.

Reject the short-termism that pervades every aspect of your life.

Look out beyond the now and realise that anything of true value takes time. And to do that demands perspective. Look up and out.

You've regained some control, you've started to develop mental and emotional discipline and started to think beyond the next five minutes. So before you have logged some kilometres or worried about the weights, you are already reaping benefits, crafting skills and behaviours that will literally serve you every minute of every day.

All because in a society where strength and discipline are no longer a necessity, you chose them anyway. A powerful act of quiet rebellion.

LESSON 4 - SUMMARY

1. Choose the hard road – In a society where we are spoiled for choice, the easy option is too often the default one. You must make the conscious choice to choose the harder road, the right road for your goals, for yourself, for your capacity to be the best version of yourself for those around you.

    It is time to get comfortable with being uncomfortable.

2. Discipline is your superpower – Motivation is cool and looks great on a poster, but the stayers, the winners, those that go the distance always have discipline. In everything they do. How you do anything is how you do everything. It's not great, it's not flashy, but it will put you above the pack time and again. So stay the course.

3. Play the long game – You know the deal, anything of true value, of real worth, takes time. There is no quick fix, simple pill, five-minute abs – you know this. So stop pretending that the answer is quick and easy. You're better than that. Play the long game and reap what you sow, long after those who chased the quick fix are left still chasing it over and over and over again.

LESSON 5

Roll with the punches

'Everybody has a plan until they get punched in the face.'
Mike Tyson

WHEN I STOOD ON THAT FROZEN start line in March 2017, ice and stone crunching underfoot, I felt well prepared. I had trained and planned and prepped. Beautifully detailed and colour coded excel spreadsheets set out my nutrition plan, pacing strategy, goal times for in and out of key checkpoints. On paper it was a veritable masterpiece. On paper.

I had planned and prepared with exquisite detail for what I had expected.

What I encountered was something very different.

I had been metaphorically punched in the face.

THE RISKS OF SPECIFICITY

It's almost like there are two checklists that you need to work off – and one of them is hidden. The one in plain view is what you would expect – using a race like the 6633 for example, it covers the logical points: physical prep, training, pacing, equipment, nutrition, logistics and so forth. All reasonable and necessary. But it is the hidden list that makes all the difference, that's the list that actually matters when the excrement makes contact with the small rotating propeller blades and the law of uneven distribution takes hold.

I felt well prepared because I had addressed that visible list. I had studiously ticked off the necessary items – ability to haul heavy sleds long distances, suitable clothing for -40c or worse, sufficient calories, water carrying capacity, solar panel to charge all those 'essential' gadgets, food plan, pace plan, blister tape, copious amounts of anti-chafe cream. I had trained specifically – specifically for what I had expected to encounter, what I had read about from previous racers, seen on YouTube, read on blogs and learned from past cold-weather experience. The great risk of specificity is that it can potentially leave you without the one key tool that you will need. The tool that will make all the difference when what you are experiencing suddenly bears no resemblance to what you had expected.

That tool is adaptability. To be more precise – it is the capacity to be mentally and emotionally flexible in the face of the uncertain, unknown or unexpected. If I was forced to identify the one single factor that made the greatest difference between my first and second attempts at the 6633 it would be that – the ability to quickly and calmly adapt.

THE HIDDEN CHECKLIST

That hidden checklist is all about the grey. There is no black and white, clear definitions, project milestones or target dates. It's all amorphous and ephemeral. It's all about the soft skills needed for hard times.

Item 1 – Develop the capacity to adapt. Quickly, calmly and effectively.

Item 2 – There is no item 2.

That's it. Learn to bend and sway and flex – to roll and tumble and rise and keep moving. To adjust, to recalculate, to compensate and recalibrate. Which all sounds cool in theory but how exactly does one build a skill that is so individual, so subjective yet so essential?

The answer is this – you train it the same way you train any skill. With practice, patience and a plan. Here's how I tackled it.

Mental, physical, emotional – these were the three realms I would need to have deep reserves and capacity in if I had any chance of finishing this race. Not winning it, the goal was simply to finish. Given that statistically I had a roughly one-in-five chance of actually making the finish line (based on the average dropout rate of competitors over the preceding decade), simply finishing seemed like more than enough of a goal.

PHYSICAL CAPACITY

The physical aspect leans heavily on the first checklist – you know the loads and distances and times and environment. So train accordingly

– with one major caveat. Don't train for what you expect, train well beyond it. Prime example – my plan was to ensure that my sled didn't weigh more than 22kg so I trained with an average load of 44kg. This ticked two boxes – one on each checklist. On that visual checklist I had ticked off capacity to haul a sled with the expected load, on that second hidden checklist I had built capacity to haul at least double what I expected. That meant that come race day, if for whatever reason my sled suddenly weighted more than planned – no factor. Physically I could simply absorb that extra load while simultaneously not trouble myself mentally or emotionally with the cost. I had seen people at the start line and early stages of the race in clear concern and even anguish over how heavy their sled felt now it was fully laden with food, fuel and water for the long hauls before them. To me, fully loaded, it felt somewhat light. Don't get me wrong, you haul that thing through a decent snow fall or up and over the Richardson Range and you definitely know it's there – but it's not a nagging, gnawing concern or trouble – it's just part and parcel.

(As a strange side note – it's fascinating, at least to me, how your own mind can utilise logic to completely lie to you. A large section of the race occurs on the frozen Peel River as we head towards the Arctic Ocean. As a river (water) it, by default, must be flat. Water doesn't run uphill, so if you are on the frozen surface of the river you are on flat ground. What happens though is that over time your mind 'forgets' that there is a sled attached and trundling along behind you. It does however register that walking seems to be harder than normal – it reconciles those two facts – I'm walking unladen but it feels harder than it should be – with a simple explanation, I must be walking uphill. To add insult to injury, your mind then interprets what your eyes are seeing with this 'uphill' explanation in mind. There were times, especially in the early dark hours, when the sleep deprivation was really starting to bite, that I would look up and would have sworn that the Peel River was not only heading north towards the Arctic Ocean but it was doing it by heading up a very steep hill. Even though there still existed the small scientific part of my mind that stated that very clearly this was an impossibility – I still saw a tough rise before me, a low gear, steep gradient climb that would have to be dealt with.)

Bottom line: you need to develop a deep reserve and capacity, a physical toolkit as complete as possible. Ticking off the minimum requirements is not enough. Turning up in 'pretty good' shape is not enough. It means looking beyond the obvious and deep diving on what lies beneath. If you've spent all your training time developing this magnificent engine – that won't help you if your chassis falls apart three days deep into the Arctic, a couple of hundred kilometres from the start and even further from the finish. Have you addressed all those underlying niggles and restrictions that you've just ignored or put down to 'advancing years' for so long? Do you know how to perform basic maintenance on your own body? Sure you know how to jump start your car, or change a tyre, but do you know what to do if your ankle seizes up, if your lower back is screaming at you, if your hip flexors have decided to suddenly shorten and stage a mutiny. Can you strap it, bandage it, glue it, splint it or straighten it? Your body is a machine – the most important one you will ever own – spend some time to understand the basics and how to deal with simple maintenance. The bonus in all of this is that these skills and capacities will serve you ad infinitum. You don't have to be about to embark some epic adventure – everyday life is more than capable of throwing you sufficient curve balls that that physical reserve and toolkit of knowledge will serve you over and over. It's worth the time so do the work.

MENTAL CAPACITY

The mental aspect can be a little more nuanced. It takes a greater degree of self-awareness and willingness to expose yourself to discomfort and difficulty, to perhaps confront some truths about your performance and the shortfalls. In reflecting on my 2017 attempt it became clear that despite my level of experience, the nights had been a particular point of weakness. They had for many of the competitors but my reality was the only one I was concerned with. The cold, the isolation, my unexpected inability to see clearly, the fact that your entire world can often be reduced to the meagre cone of light cast out from your head torch – all conspire to remind you of how small and fragile you are and how vast and uncompromising this environment was. I needed to change that narrative. I made the decision to flip that script and make nights my time to shine – a time of the day that I would excel, make distance, stay strong and thrive. To that end, I moved a great deal of my training into the dark. I'd head out for long training sessions and watch the sun go down knowing that I'll be in the dark until the job got done. Set the alarm for some dire and entirely uncivilised hour in the dead of night so I could get up and go hit the trails. Do it over and over and over until the night it not just somewhere I was comfortable but somewhere I was happy. Somewhere I could thrive. By the time I stood on the start line in 2019 I no longer feared the nights. I looked forward to them.

This is about taking the time to do some very honest reflection on your performance. See the gaps for what they are and rather than try to explain them away or rail against them – recognise them, neither as good nor bad, but simply as something that needs to be addressed and then set out a plan to deal with it. One of the greatest aspects with mental training is that you can (and are) doing it every waking moment. It's not like trying to make time for an hour in the gym or some time to go for a run – every decision you make, those myriad small choices every day, are part of the tapestry of mental training. Take the escalators or the stairs, get up early or sleep in, walk or drive, easy or hard, fast or slow, good enough or done right. Every choice, every decision point is building mental muscle memory. 'Greasing the groove', as famous Russian kettlebell aficionado Pavel Tsatsouline would put it, building (or eroding) that mental resolve and resilience so that when the times come that do require the hard choices, your default position is one of strength and capacity – not defence and weakness.

EMOTIONAL CAPACITY

The last cornerstone on my hidden checklist was emotional capacity. Being starkly realistic, I had to accept that at some point (or points) during this race I would buckle under the onslaught. It's like a three pronged attack – the environment wears on you physically, your body is incinerating calories far faster than you can shovel them in so metabolically your reserves are constantly dwindling, and you're alone and exposed and very far from home. Loved ones are literally on the other side of the planet, almost as far away as geographically possible. At some point you are going to have to find a way to deal with being emotionally and physically driven to your knees. How would I tackle this? Like any true nerd – with science.

I would game 'the system'. Part of my training strategy for 2019 involved breath work – not only around how it impacted my aerobic capacity but also how it impacted my body biochemically and therefore emotionally. What are emotions if not manifestations of the chemical balances and imbalances swirling within us at any given moment? This is a very deep rabbit hole and one that is well beyond the scope of this book - but the bottom line is this – with a grasp of some of the basic tenets of how your body works, along with some training, you can take a measure of control over your emotions. In this specific case I was working on using my breath as a tool – the cadence, measure and force to actively influence the levels of carbon dioxide and oxygen in my system at any given time. How did that help? Imagine someone gave you a magic black box with a dial on it and you could use that dial to control the 'revs' on the engine that is your nervous system. Need to ramp up output, get the fires stoked, ready for a push then turn up the dial (in practice by utilising some specific cadenced breath work). Need to stop and quickly turn the system down so you can grab some sleep, but then need to ramp it back up again – same process, breath work to dial it down, different work to ramp it up. Exponents of yoga and certain corners of the sporting community will not be surprised at this process at all, to some it may even seem self-evident, but through my experience, and for the vast majority of people, the concept of utilising something as simple and seemingly 'invisible' as the manner in which we breathe to take a great measure of control over your physical and therefore emotional state is both novel and exciting. This wasn't just about managing my athletic performance – it was also about using these tools to influence my mental and emotional state. It's rarely 'one big mistake' that takes you out of races this long – it's the wretched accumulation of a myriad small cuts. The capacity to keep a positive mental state in the face of that onslaught is what separates the wheat from the chaff. When the dark became oppressive and my sled harness broke and then I spilt my last hot choc powder, which I'd been saving for the last 12 hours – that's when I would use my breath to take back control and slow it all down. To seek some clarity and revert to my usual adage in those situations – find the problem, fix the problem. Calmly and efficiently deal with the most pressing matter first and then move to the next. Solve enough problems and you get the job done. But you can't do that when the emotions are in turmoil and the mind has been relegated to the backseat as the chemicals drive the system to overload.

LESSON 5 - SUMMARY

1. Build a deep and broad physical capacity beyond what you think will be required.

2. Be brutally honest about where you are weak and solve that problem.

3. Do the honest, hard, uncomfortable work. Be happy about it. Find peace and comfort within it.

4. Understand how you function as a human being and learn how to take charge of that system.

Then pack up your toolkit and go to 'war'.
Get the job done.

LESSON 6
The mind makes it real

'If a person gave away your body to a passer-by you'd be furious, yet you hand over your mind to anyone that comes along so that they may abuse you, leaving you troubled and disturbed – have you no shame in that?'

Epictetus

Neo: I thought it wasn't real
Morpheus: Your mind makes it real
Matrix

I COULD LAY OUT ANY NUMBER of amazing training plans for you, point you in the direction of master coaches and subject-matter experts for the preparation of your body for an endeavour like this, but it would all be for naught if we neglected to harden the greatest and most dangerous tool in your arsenal – your mind.

There has to come an acceptance that at some point your mind will engage in acts of self-sabotage in a bid to save your body from what it perceives as impending damage and potential annihilation. The great central governor theory proposes that your body sets a 'tolerance thermostat' – and if you are pushing that limit it will pull you back, regardless of what capacity lies in the tank. At some point, despite you being capable of much more, your mind will try to apply the handbrake – unless you train yourself to do otherwise. This is the difference between those that can and those that can't. 'Those that can' seem to have some unnatural level of control over their body – the sheer will to drive it beyond what would seem to be normal limits of reason. Most of us would happily step back from this line, but these people will leap over and drive on.

You have to see your mind for what it is – a masterful tool and potentially your greatest weakness. Like any tool you must learn to use it correctly and efficiently. You must hone it and sharpen it and care for it. You must work diligently to become cognisant of those weaknesses and learn how to manage them, to ameliorate them, to see them for what they are. There are any number of books espousing the manner in which we can achieve this but bottom line – it's a personal journey. What works for some doesn't work for others, or it works to different degrees and with varying results. For what it's worth, I do think there are some underlying truths and I will share here how I approached the tricky art of building the level of mental resilience I thought would be necessary for an undertaking of this magnitude. The advantage being that mental resilience serves you no matter the circumstance – I knew that time invested here would pay dividends long after the race was over. How could you not do the work required when the benefits and payoff were both long lasting and substantial?

Here are the corner stones of how I tackled building the mind as opposed to solely the body.

1. DO THE WORK

I know I use this catchphrase somewhat relentlessly but it is an unavoidable truth. At some point you just have to do the work. The discipline and confidence that comes with the knowledge that you have truly done the hard physical prep work is invaluable and irreplaceable. It cannot be substituted with any other belief or training – you must know deep down in your soul that you have done the work. Any shortcuts, any weakness has the risk of resurfacing in that internal dialogue when the road is getting tough. If you know that you have not cut a single corner and are ready for whatever comes, it becomes slightly easier to keep that internal dialogue strong. In training I did not short a single rep, miss a single kilometre, skimp a single kilogram. Ever. Period. These were crucial yet minuscule daily decisions and actions in the weeks and months of preparation – but they were building a mental fortress brick by brick, a fortress that would become unassailable in the hard times ahead. Therein, to some degree, lies the beauty – to build something so powerful, so insurmountable, you need only make small, consistent, correct decisions day in and out. It is the split-second behaviour and choices that build the ramparts. Once you see that all you need is the smallest of steps, to not skimp here, to shortcut there, or just do one less, or accept a little reduction – then it becomes easier. Make the right choice, every time. No matter how small or insignificant it may seem – those choices are not simply decision points, they are repetitions in your training and they must be countless and perfect if you wish to reap the rewards – and importantly, not waste your time.

2. VISUALISATION

Powerful, yes, but it must be 'realistic'. My experience has been that the real value in visualisations comes in seeing the task being realistically hard even brutally hard, rather than it seeing it as being 'easy' because you are so good. You need honest 'hard road' visualisations rather than 'triumphant hero' moments. Then when the truth comes knocking and it is hard, or you do suffer setbacks, you are not left suddenly doubting your own self-imposed status as 'all conquering hero' but realise that while the road is long and hard, you are capable of rising to the challenge.

3. AUTOPILOT

I thought of this as 'autopilot' but others may think of this more in the sense of meditation, and the comparison is valid.

When the challenge is physical, having that deeply crafted muscle memory and allowing the body to pretty much go on autopilot can be lifesaving. In the days ahead during the race, my sleep deprivation would become so extreme I literally felt that it was simply muscle memory and sheer determination that kept me moving. I reached a point where I was hallucinating my entire surroundings (I thought I was in a dense forest for a full night when in fact I was in the middle of a pretty much endless white ice sheet) and was blacking-out every 50 steps or so but somehow simply kept getting up and stumbling on until the sun came up and my mind would allow me to be somewhat awake. But that skill comes from repetition in all manner of environments – I would train awake, exhausted, day, night, 3pm, 3am, so that the mechanics of the race were simply automatic regardless of everything else. You must train not just your body but your mind to accept that we simply need to 'flip the switch' and go. We don't need to have some deep conscious discussion or consider alternatives or delay – we simply need to do, as if it was all an autonomic spinal reflex rather than conscious decision. Leave the ego out and let the mind simply drive the machine.

How did I know if I had achieved this capacity of autopilot? There were sections of the race where I didn't think about anything, I felt as if I didn't even think. There was literally no conscious thought other than the recognition of my own foot falls and the passing of the tundra. There would be later parts of the race where I had very little recollection, if any, of sections I passed through.

4. FRAMEWORKS – MENTAL AND PHYSICAL

You need some structures to fall back on. The mental framework is having a very deep understanding of why you are doing this, a very clear plan as well as comfort for adapting if/when the plan falls apart. The physical is a process/skill you can use to manage the physiology of emotions more than anything. For me that was learning to use breathwork to up or down regulate as required as well as being relentlessly self-aware of how I was travelling. Find the problem, fix the problem. Daily self-check – how's the body, feet, legs, hips etc? How's my temperature, hydration, caloric intake? How is my mood, what is my internal dialogue, what am I thinking about? What needs attention – have a drink, fix that blister, sing a silly song to lift my mood?

5. RUTHLESS EFFICIENCY

Compound interest has been described as the ninth wonder of the world – and this is the compounding interest of small victories across the entirety of the race. It often seems like silly stuff to some people but I trained everything for that race so I could be ruthlessly efficient. In this case it meant I could change clothes, make food, eat, clean and prep meals, all while not breaking stride or having to get out of my harness. That efficiency pays dividends at the front end in terms of energy preservation, it pays long term in being able to still execute the required task even on autopilot and lastly it gives you great mental strength to know that you have your shit well and truly dialled in. Know where every piece of kit is, replace it where it should be – every time, don't leave zips open, don't tolerate a loose strap or poorly repacked piece of equipment. Accept nothing less than the required perfection and discipline. To accept anything less is to rob yourself, no one else, and why would you steal from yourself when you have sacrificed so much and committed so deeply to being here?

6. INTERNAL DIALOGUE

Be ruthless in eliminating negative thoughts. During the race I would always tell myself – and any race officials I came across – that I was great, travelling really well, happy, warm, etc. There will be times when the walls crack a little and that's when the mental framework comes in – one aspect of my framework was knowing that I would not get another chance to attempt this race so it had to get done. Given that, it was getting done regardless – I could do the miles happy or miserable, but they would get done. So you may as well cheer up buttercup. That's not to say I was a Terminator style robot every day – there were times when the pity party crept in, when the tears flowed, the shoulders slumped. You are indeed only human – but the default position has to be one of realisation of what is happening and how you are responding and then getting the train back on the tracks. You must stand up and dust off. The ability to do that is predicated on all the points above. They do not necessarily stand alone, but dovetail to form an impenetrable phalanx.

> 'To make a deep physical path we walk again and again and again. To make a deep mental path, we must think over and over the kind of thoughts we wish to dominate our lives.'
> *Henry David Thoreau*

7. SEE NOT THE MOUNTAIN, ONLY ITS PARTS

This particular piece of Gesaltism comes from my mountaineering days and was one of the most important pieces of advice I was ever given. If you stand at the beginning of the expedition and look up at the summit it is all too easy to look at the vastness of the endeavour before you, the sheer magnitude of it all, and allow yourself to entertain those doubtful thoughts – how the hell am I ever going to do this? That is the first step on the slippery downward slope that leads to mental capitulation and eventual failure.

Instead, see only the immediate task before you – what do I need to do to get to the next break, the next kilometre, to midday, to camp, to the end of the day? Task by task, deal with each in turn and they will mount up, success after minor success. Before you know it you will have scaled the vast majority of the mountain and only the final day will remain.

One step at a time. That is how every single race is won. It's how everything is done.

All in all, how does all that manifest in the real world? Here's a little jump forward in time to 2019 and my return to the 6633, as I made my way into the checkpoint at Inuvik. I wrote about it in a blog post a few months after I returned but here is an excerpt with some added context addressing the points above.

"I remember vividly the exact moment the booming voice of legendary SEAL and Echelon Front CEO, Jocko Willink came thundering from the clouds above, drove itself like a bolt of lightning launched by Zeus himself deep into my cranium – his

words filling every corner of my fatigued and frozen brain pan. The problem was simple and as with so many simple problems, the solution was just as eloquent.

I was dragging a sled on the frozen Peel River, heading into Inuvik. I had been racing non-stop for over 120 hours, five days, battered by katabatic winds, plummeting temperatures and crippling sleep deprivation. But Inuvik was a shining light – the second last checkpoint in a 614km race, the only checkpoint that was indoors with a functioning shower no less. It would be my one and only shower in what would be almost 200 consecutive hours of exposure to the Arctic elements. The problem I thought I was getting close, really close, this stage was 120km long, over 30 hours of grinding through ice and snow since the last checkpoint, and as I saw the photographer's car approach I knew that it could only be a measly few kilometres away. Weronika, an Inuvik local, slowed as she drove past and I asked her the one question I shouldn't have.

'How far to the checkpoint?'

'Ten miles.'

'Are you sure?' I asked, as my heart sunk through my feet, the ice and finally settled into the silt at the bottom of the Peel River. Are you sure? Like she might be wrong, because she lives here...and had an odometer in her car, you know, like she had no idea about her own backyard.

Ten miles (16km) doesn't sound like much, but when you've been dragging that damn sled for almost 450km already and ten kilometres means hours of more work, not minutes, when you are desperate to stop and sleep, if only for an hour, a glorious hour, then ten kilometres may as well be fifty.

That's when Jocko arrived. If you haven't heard Jocko's voice, imagine Charlton Heston and Sam Elliot had a love child, and that child grew up on a strict diet of whiskey, Fred Flintstone sized tomahawk steaks and the tears of vanquished foes. You get the drift.

'You know what I do when I have a task or job that I hate and am desperate to avoid…I do it harder.'

Truth delivered like a hammer blow on the anvil of my self-pity, he rapidly departed. And I realised that I had a choice.

Do the kilometres and complain, trudging along like the weight of the world had arrived to personally ruin my day. Or…I could laugh and slap those ten kilometres so hard they wouldn't wake up until next week (which ironically sounded great, sleeping for a week that is, not so much the slap...) So I took a moment, breathed, stretched and then started power walking like a crazed Olympian on the home stretch without fear of disqualification if the odd step looks a bit more like a jog than a walk. Oddly enough the fatigue lifted just slightly, the sun seemed a little warmer and as I marched and chased down those last kilometres to the checkpoint I found myself in a good mood."

That mood would serve me well long after that moment had passed, it was really a mental turning point for me, although I didn't know it at the time.

LESSON 6 - SUMMARY

The greatest tool within your toolkit resides between your ears. Here's how to keep it sharp and charged.

1. Do the Work – Period. No quarter. Just do the damn work.

2. Visualisation – Be realistic, don't imagine it being easy and you simply walking it in, imagine it being hard as hell and you overcoming no matter what comes your way.

3. Autopilot – Sometimes you need to be able to turn off the noise and pain and doubt and chatter and just let the body you have crafted get the work done.

4. Frameworks – mental and physical. Know why you are here, why this is important to you and have actionable strategies for dealing with the inevitable bumps in the road.

5. Ruthless Efficiency – How you do anything is how you do everything. Be ruthless.

6. Internal Dialogue – As the old adage goes, if you think you can or think you can't, you're probably right.

7. See Not the Whole Mountain – One step at a time. That's how you climb everything. No matter the size.

part three

GO HUNGRY & COLD LIKE THE WOLF (SECOND ATTEMPT AT 6633 ARCTIC ULTRA)

CHAPTER 11
Arctic Circle

Day 1

Eagle Plains (start line) to Arctic Circle (CP1)

Section distance: 36km

Section time: 6 hrs 33 mins

Time at CP: 30 mins

Total distance: 36km

Total time: 7 hrs 03 mins

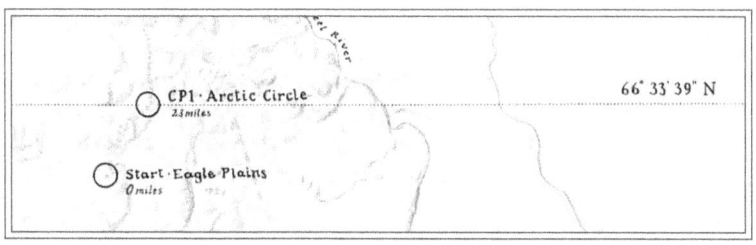

YOU KNOW WHAT IS COMING – the hills, the cold, the pain, the sleep deprivation. All of that is not only out there waiting for you but it is in there in your mind, whispering, reminding you that it is all lurking, in the wild expanse, in the dark nights, stacked heavily before those seemingly elusive sunrises.

It was a blessing in many ways. Finally all the questions would be laid to rest. The training would be put the test, the will would be put to anvil and I would see how malleable I was.

I headed out to the start line and settled myself at the back of the field. As I lifted my harness and settled in, tightened straps, adjusted layers of clothing, a slow and steady calm came over me. I could stop dreaming about it – I was here. It was time.

I had positioned myself up the back as I had a very clear plan. I knew the exact pace I would hit from here to the first checkpoint. I knew the terrain, what was ahead and how I would tackle it. I didn't care if my pace left me dead last or somewhere in the middle. It was my pace, my plan and I would brook no dissent, we would hold the plan.

Three.

Two.

One.

Go.

So it begins. My body did exactly what it was trained to do. I settled straight into my pace and headed out onto the Dempster Highway into the Yukon. Very quickly it became apparent that with the exception of some of the fast competitors in the 193 km race and the three racing competitors in the 614 km race – Avram, Didier and Patrick – who appeared clearly out for the win, my pace was actually one of the faster ones out there. Within the first five or so kilometres I had moved from the very back of the field to the front end of the main pack. Two years ago that would have worried me, that I was going too fast too early, this time there was no such concerns in my mind. I was sticking to my plan and that plan put me here, so be it.

I was travelling with a British competitor, David Smale, for much of the next thirty kilometres or so, as our pace and position were very similar. This surprised me because in 2017 David (a veteran of the race) had left me way behind, his pace then was something that was well beyond me.

In 2017 I remember being plagued with insecurities during this section as people would pass me or catch up to me. Those thoughts playing in your mind – are you too slow? Is everyone else in another league compared to you? What are you doing here? Now the inner dialogue was positive, disciplined and one that allowed me to actually enjoy this first section.

The weather was unseasonably warm by Yukon Arctic standards, around -5 to -10C. Which sounds like a reprieve but for some turned out to be a curse. The 'warmer' temperature and physical exertion left some competitors scrambling to get their layering right – too much and you start to sweat, as soon as you stop the sweat freezes and you are now wearing a suit of ice – hypothermia is suddenly a very serious risk. For me it was simply part of the race to deal with, years of mountain climbing in freezing cold places had left me with an almost innate understanding of how to constantly adjust layering and control body temperature. Zips on layers fly up and down over and over, beanies come on and off, on and off as I adjusted on the run.

The trail dropped down over the first 8km to Engineer Creek and then I knew it was pretty much rolling hills, with an overall steady ascent, all the way to CP 1 at the line of the Arctic Circle. Both David and I rolled into CP1 slightly behind the front runners and well in front of the rest of the pack – which was ideal. No queues of athletes all trying to get thermoses filled, it was relatively calm and quiet.

It was here that I played probably my first psychological move for the race. No particular reason but some part of me must have known that I was tackling this on a far more strategic and competitive approach than I was consciously admitting. When athletes arrive at a checkpoint, their entry time is logged on a board for all to see, as is their exit time. So you can gauge where the people ahead of you are, what time they got here, how long they stayed and when they left. This also gives you some insight into their strategy later in the race and how they may be travelling – are they bivvying out and having short breaks at the checkpoints or pushing from one to the next and taking long recovery times at the checkpoints? A short stop would suggest strength, longer and longer breaks may suggest otherwise – potentially. So rather than head into the trailer and announce I was here and get logged in I hung back and sorted all my kit – got the thermos out, tidied up a few loose items in my sled and then headed in. This way my log in and out times would be very close together. Even though I spent around twenty minutes there, anyone behind me could look at the log and it would appear that I was there for only a few minutes before heading out again.

This section was really a warm-up physically and mentally for me, now we were heading into the first real test – the first night on the trail. In 2017 this first night had been a brutal rite of passage that spat me out the next morning. It had claimed several victims that year and while I survived, it had certainly put a serious dent in my aspirations and well and truly knocked some of the sass right out of me. Time to see how the 'new me' would fare.

CHAPTER 12
James Creek

Arctic Circle (CP1) to James Creek (CP2)

Section distance: 78km

Section time: 18 hrs 30 mins

Time at CP: 2 hrs 10 mins

Total distance: 114km

Total time: 27 hrs 43 mins

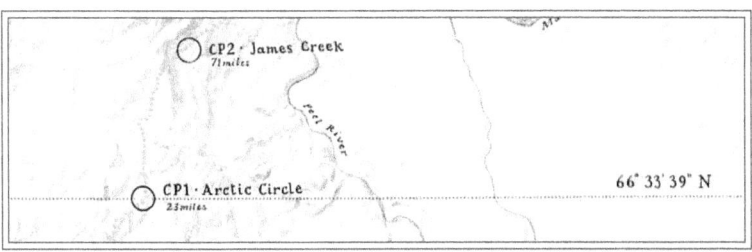

THIS IS THE SECTION THAT I wanted to get behind me as quickly as possible. Two main reasons – it's via Wrights Pass, where a vast majority of the 'hills' live, and it's notorious for sudden and violent changes in the weather. You may recall that the climb up to Wrights Pass, the highest point of the entire race at 953m above sea level, is 'affectionately' known as 'Hurricane Alley'. It's a lurking ground for katabatic winds capable of picking up a full grown person and literally throwing them off the trail. In 2018 a sudden storm had swept through catching the middle and rear sections of the pack, the front runners were left unscathed but much of the rear echelon had to be extracted from the course at speed for their own safety – even then it was no easy matter with the winds simply picking up sleds (and those attached to them) and hurling them across the highway into waiting snow banks.

My plan was to push straight through from the start line all the way to CP2 at James Creek in a single stint – no stopping for a rest or bivvy. Get the hills and risky weather windows behind me and then take a break. In 2017 it had taken me just shy of 21 hours to make the journey from CP1 to CP2 – the plan this time was to shave that down considerably. And shave it I did. I was still travelling with David at this point – we were both keeping our own independent pace, which meant we would regularly swap positions of who was in front of who, but always be within a few hundred metres of each other. I found this quite enjoyable – I was still relatively on my own but had the slight comfort of someone to chat to from time to time as we passed each other. Neither of us were under any illusions that we were racing each other, there was simply the camaraderie of the trail and the quiet enjoyment of the stunning landscape we were in.

The sun swept down to my left, dipping below the horizon, bringing with it beautiful swathes of pink across the sky. It also took with it the last vestiges of any semblance of warmth – both physical and psychological. The trail north at this stage was fairly straight and roughly thirty kilometres from CP1 we hit the point known as Rock River Campground. Rock River had previously been a kind of halfway unofficial checkpoint, a spot to potentially grab some warm water if the support trailer was in residence and often a point for people to bivvy up and grab some sleep. This year there was no support vehicles here, we had been warned that we would be completely on our own until CP2.

Given the 'somewhat warm' weather – it was roughly -15C, both David and I decided to take a very short break at Rock River, tend to some admin, calls of nature and grab a meal. A quick transfer of hot water from a thermos into a freeze-dried meal bag and ten minutes later I was ready to head off and have a very late night dinner on the run. Nothing like some Hawaiian Chicken with Pineapple at 12:30am. I did discover the hard way however that if you are impatient and don't sufficiently mix up your meal and then wait the requisite amount of time – you end up spending the next ten to fifteen minutes spitting out solid chunks of freeze-dried pineapple – less than ideal but lesson learnt. Over the next few hours David opened up a slight lead on me. The next 20km was all uphill, taking us all the way to the top of Wrights Pass.

Around 4am the fact that I had been on my feet holding a solid pace for the last 18 hours started to make itself known. Nothing major, just that first stage of push back as the mind and body probed and pushed for a decent rest and a sleep – neither of which were on the agenda. In the end a compromise was reached, I stopped, made a thermos of coffee and allowed myself a five-minute rest, sitting on my sled and drinking my coffee. A quick chat with myself – out loud – about it being ok to 'grab a five' and celebrate the fact that we were off to a cracker start. Not to mention that we were about to tackle the climb up and over the Pass. I had desperately wanted to do that climb in the dark – for no other purpose than it helps keep you focused on nothing other than the trail that lies illuminated in the small circle cast by your head torch.

The northern side of the Pass is typically where the wind lurks and the weather lies in wait for the weary athlete, but this night obviously that message hadn't come through. The last five kilometres of unforgiving, winding route up the mountain was besieged by heavy winds, whipping up the snow and turning anything small and fine off the trail into an airborne abrasive. Looking up ahead I could see the small light of David's head torch inching its way up towards the Pass in the dark. I took a moment to fish out a pair of prescription wrap around glasses – they sit somewhere between regular glasses and full snow goggles, giving me clear vision but cutting out a majority of the wind that was busy trying to freeze my eyeballs. Then it was head down and grind all the way uphill.

I made slow, relentless progress as the early hours of the morning slowly slipped away. Finally as the pink hues of pre-dawn crept up from the east I cleared the final set of false summits and topped out over the pass. Psychologically this was a big tick. The hardest single climb of the entire 614km course was now behind me – as was the first night – and I had ticked off two big ticket items. I had come through the first night in solid form and had cleared the Pass. I celebrated the dawn with a bag of freeze-dried raspberry granola – chosen for no other reason than the staggering amount of calories, 1200 calories per bag. It warmed the belly as I started the descent off the Pass and worked on chopping down the last 20km to James Creek and CP2. The winds had abated somewhat and it was simply a case of chewing up the distance. It was on this section, in the early dawn light that a support vehicle had come past and I noticed my fellow Aussie compatriot Matt Size in the back seat – one of the casualties of the night. Matt was no stranger to the race but a stomach condition rendering him unable to hold down fluids or food for the last 24 hours had made the race simply an untenable risk for him to go forward. I was gutted for him but knew I would see him at each CP going forward, and with his humour and sarcasm he would be a welcome sight at every one of them.

The plan was to take a decent break at James Creek (CP2) and try to grab maybe a few hours sleep. I estimated I would have been on the go for well over 24 hours by the time I arrived and still had exactly 500km to go.

I rolled into James Creek at 11am on Friday morning, 24 hours and 30 minutes since I had left the start line. But more importantly I had covered that total distance seven hours faster than I had in 2017. Literally only one day in and already I had carved seven hours off my previous time. Which of course left me wondering – was that because I had been monumentally slow last time or was I really that much quicker this time. Only time would tell.

CHAPTER 13

Fort McPherson

James Creek (CP2) to Fort McPherson (CP3)

Section distance: 68km

Section time: 19 hrs 57 mins

Time at CP: 5 hrs 6 mins

Total distance: 182km

Total time: 51 hrs 46 mins

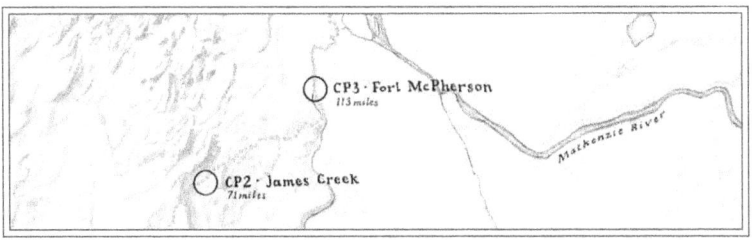

JAMES CREEK IS A HEAVY MACHINERY depot where the Roads Department operate their heavy duty clearing equipment. Huge snow ploughs and heavy haulage trucks filled the shed. The heater was blasting away making it incredibly hot after coming in from the literally Arctic conditions outside. And to add to the ambience the CB radio was on full loudspeaker, alerting the crews if any transports on the road were in trouble and needed assistance. Being in trouble generally meant being buried in a snowbank or simply locked into a huge snow drift in the middle of the highway – this was not a thoroughfare for the faint hearted.

I always spent the last few kilometres coming into a checkpoint mentally running through in my mind what I needed to do, the best order in which to do things and what the plan for pack up and exit was. It not only helped to stave off fatigue but also, more importantly, it ensured I didn't waste precious time and energy once I arrived and when I was leaving. Historically I had been a chronic time waster at checkpoints – I had made a conscious effort to rid myself of this fault in every race since.

Arriving at 11am on Friday morning, I now had the majority of the hills and riskiest weather window behind me. The harness came off, I quickly grabbed my bivvy bag, a power bank to recharge my watches – I had two watches, Suunto Spartan Ultra for tracking race data (pace, hours elapsed, etc) and a Suunto Ambit 3 Peak for time/date (it was very easy to quickly lose all sense of what time of day it was and then simply what day it actually was anyway) and no I'm not sponsored by Suunto I just have a long history of using their products in extreme environments and they have never failed me. I headed into the main garage to claim some 'prime real estate' amongst the heavy machinery on the diesel-stained concrete floor. Once my bed was set I headed back out to drop off my thermoses with the support crew, I asked them to fill them up in about two hours. I filled up a freeze-dried meal to eat in 'bed' before grabbing some sleep. Back in the garage I stripped off a few layers and hung them over some of the machinery in the hope of airing and drying them a little.

Real sleep proved to be maddeningly elusive. Partly because of the seemingly oppressive heat of the garage and the CB radio, apparently at maximum volume, blaring into life at random intervals as trucks on the Dempster either checked in or chatted away the long miles. After about ninety minutes of fitful dozing, I decided that I would be better out on the trail and could grab some sleep in the open later on. It was still the middle of the day and moving during the daylight hours was always a more pleasant experience than the psychological and emotional challenge of forging forward in the dark.

I asked David when he was planning on heading out as I thought we would continue to travel together – turns out his feet were beginning to macerate and without serious time drying out they would inevitably blister up over the coming kilometres leaving him with no other choice but to call it quits before any serious damage was done.

This left me to head out on my own – and that would be the theme for the majority of the remaining 500km of the race. With the exception of a few hours here and there I would spend the rest of the race entirely alone. I grabbed my thermoses, ate some more food and at 13:50hrs departed James Creek on the road to cover the 68km to the First Nation hamlet of Fort McPherson.

From a racing and strategy point of view, Fort Mac was a big deal – at least it was to me. Several key things happened there. First, it was where the 193 km race concluded, leaving us with fewer competitors on the trail. It was also the point where we could pick up our first drop bag, resupplying and providing an opportunity to unload and drop off any kit we decided was superfluous. Lastly, after Fort McPherson, as we were departing the Dempster Highway and heading onto the ice road, the race organisers were happy for us to use earphones to listen to music etc. if we wanted to. I hadn't planned on it but having the option was welcome. We would also be saying goodbye to the Dempster at Fort Mac and dropping onto the winding Peel River – beautiful but much more likely to be colder as we were little lower down and on a frozen highway of water.

There was a steep climb out of James Creek but I knew this was the last serious one for a very long time, literally hundreds of kilometres. While the trail was undulating the net result of this section was that we would drop from James Creek at 645m above sea level, down to Fort McPherson at a lowly 7m. Even the terrain was changing – no longer surrounded by mountains and steep landscape, the vista opened up to reveal vast swathes of tundra and rolling low hills. We were truly descending down into the Northwest Territories of far northern Canada.

Around 5pm I noted that the first auditory hallucinations began to appear. In 2017 hallucinations had been a hallmark of my second and third nights on the trail and they had been heralded in the same way – hearing things that weren't there. In this case I kept thinking I could hear a radio, very quiet but present, in the background – almost as if it was playing over my shoulder from somewhere behind me on the trail. I knew what was going on, made a note in my race diary and kept charging along.

As the sun began to set it was time to try to catch some of that sleep that had been so elusive at James Creek. Before leaving James

Creek I had asked David about good bivvy points between there and Fort McPherson – David's knowledge of the area was nothing short of spectacular. He mentioned MidWay Lake Campground and a rough distance from here to there so I would find it. Sure enough in the dark hours of the evening I came across a sign for MidWay Lake. What I didn't come across was a sign for the campground – I found an unmarked 'road' which was just a path of cleared snow that was wide enough for a vehicle, which seemed to lead to absolutely nowhere. This left me with the dilemma – do I just move down this path a little and bivvy up hoping no one tries to drive in or out in the early hours, or keep moving up the trail (which was of course uphill at this point) and see if I can find another entrance or better site? I decided to move about 400m up the trail to see if I could find any other entrances. Finding nothing, I grumpily stomped back to the original path in, found the best alcove in the snow bank and threw out the bivvy.

I was tired, grumpy and just generally unimpressed with everything and everyone at this point – everyone being the sum total of me and no one else. I jumped into my sleeping bag which was thankfully reasonably 'warm' and set my alarm for two hours. Normally I would have slept for less but I was trying to make up for James Creek. To be honest I have no idea how much sleep I actually managed to get – you drift in and out of this exhausted dream state, unaware of whether you have been asleep or not – which invariably leaves you stressing over that fact that you weren't sleeping (or so you thought). My alarm sounded at the two-hour mark and in a relatively foul mood I unzipped the hood of my bivvy and angrily whipped down the hood. My mood was instantly silenced.

While I had slept/dozed/wriggled/wrestled about, the northern lights had come out in all their glory. Bright trails of luminescent green stretched across the star filled sky above me. I was silenced, humbled and received a very valuable lesson that I feel helped me quickly and permanently (in race terms) reframe my mental position. It was a stark and swift reminder to drop my attitude and take a moment to appreciate what the hell was going on. I was working my way, solo, deep into the Arctic Circle. I was travelling under what most people would regard as a once-in-a-lifetime experience – a stunning view of the northern lights. To top it off I was seeing it in a part of the world with zero light pollution from civilisation, it was unadulterated, unsullied and I was completely alone witnessing the laws of physics produce one of nature's most breathtaking phenomena.

Bivvy rolled up, harness on, back to work. A few hours further on I spotted some lights off to my right, far off in the distance. At first they left me slightly confused, my sleep-deprived mind trying to reconcile what a house, lit up at 3am in the morning was doing out here in the middle of nowhere. I remember thinking they must have been having a late night party, hence the lights at such a strange hour. Finally sanity prevailed and I realised I was looking at the lights of Fort McPherson. It was cruel comfort – those lights were tantalizing but Fort Mc was still six hours of hard work away. They remained in the distance, showing no intention of moving any closer for hours and hours as I strode on in the dark. As dawn light crept up I grabbed a quick 30-minute bivvy (in what seemed to be a random snow laden driveway) a slightly more successful break as I actually felt that I managed something approximating sleep.

As mentioned earlier, the last few hours into Fort McPherson are Machiavellian to say the least. You drop down to the Peel River ferry crossing, the temperature plummets and batters at you as you swiftly descend and charge across the frozen gateway. From there, the final approach to Fort is a seemingly never ending undulating, almost featureless, road. The town itself is hidden from view and the trail simply curves and rolls in seemingly endless turns and false summits. Once the town finally reveals itself you still have to take a left turn and walk almost the entire length of town to reach the community hall that was CP3.

It was a welcome arrival – at 181km into the race I could tuck almost a third of the total distance away 'in the bag'. I had a drop bag here with fresh supplies, a magnificently oversized Kit Kat and the opportunity to sleep in the community hall's gymnasium – a quiet, dark space that would be our last serious respite until Inuvik, well over 200km or about five full marathons away. It was also a chance to see who was here and who had moved on, typically most athletes took a solid rest here – it had been a mountainous and somewhat sleep-deprived battle to get here and while the ice road ahead was flat, it would be much colder and checkpoints far more spartan from here on out.

I arrived at Fort McPherson at 9:30am Saturday morning. This was the last CP that was on the same course that I had completed in 2017. In terms of raw hours racing,

I had arrived here over 11 hours faster than my 2017 doppelganger. In a little under two days I had already made up almost half a day. I was under no illusions that my race this year was going to be a vastly different experience to the trials and tribulations that had claimed me only two years earlier.

CHAPTER 14

Mid River

Fort McPherson (CP3) to Mid Peel River (CP4)

Section distance: 76km

Section time: 24 hrs 45 mins

Time at CP: 1hr

Total distance: 258km

Total time: 76 hrs 31 mins

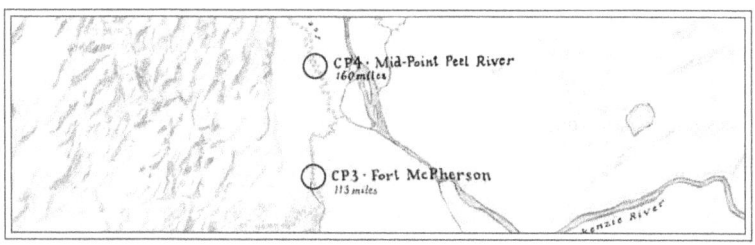

MENTALLY, AND STRATEGICALLY, I had broken the race up into four sections.

1. Start to Fort McPherson – 181km, that covered the hills, the risky

weather windows and would see the field thin out and everyone settle into their positions.

2. Fort Mac to Aklavik – 157km, it would be flat but remote, colder, exposed and potentially a very mentally tough section. You're a long way from the start and a long way from home, no-man's land for somewhere between 30 and 40 hours of racing.

3. Aklavik to Inuvik – 120km, the longest single section of the race. Getting deep into exhaustion, conditions could be unpredictable, still on the ice road, which would take a toll on the lower body – the ice would be unforgiving. Inuvik was also a beacon, psychologically. I felt if I could get into and more importantly out of Inuvik then I could do the full distance. The race, regardless of time, would be well within my grasp if I could simply stay on my feet long enough and keep moving.

4. Inuvik to Tuktoyaktuk – 158km. This was the stage of which I knew the least but was also the least concerned about. This would be 160km of hard-packed trail winding its way between the myriad frozen lakes that form the Mackenzie Delta. It would be remote, barren and beautiful. My working theory was that if I had made it this far there would be almost nothing that could stop me from reaching the finish line – even if I had to crawl.

My plan had allowed for a sizeable rest break here. I knew I would be coming in somewhat sleep deprived and depending on what the meteorological gods had metered out, I may well have been somewhat weather beaten too.

The CP at Fort Mc was indoors and spacious. It was a community hall, the front section a common room and kitchen, from there a hallway extended back towards the bathroom and into a large indoor basketball court. The court was fairly much in darkness, providing plenty of room for weary athletes to find a quiet space for a sleep.

The problem wasn't space or noise, it turned out to be heat. It felt incredibly warm, almost hot. To add to that, even though I had set myself up away from other athletes, the muscles in my legs refused to relax, they jumped and jerked and cramped. My original plan was to allow two hours for food and admin and to try to get four hours of sleep here, to recharge the batteries and give me enough to strike out hard into the next stage. After somewhere between two and three hours of fitful sleep, drifting in and out I decided to cut my losses and slowly go about getting my sled reorganised, load my thermos, raid my drop bag and get some more calories onboard.

Having arrived at 9:30am I found myself harnessed up and heading out of Fort Mc at 2:30pm that afternoon. The trail headed north on the remainder of the main road and then dropped through the stunted and sparse copses down onto the freshly ploughed ice road that would take us all the way to Aklavik. As I was heading out of a town a dog sidled up next to me. A quick look revealed a well worn collar with a chewed piece of lead hanging off it – someone had clearly gotten bored of being tied up at home and was keen for some adventure. At first I thought she would wander along for a bit, eventually get bored of me and head home. I was sorely mistaken.

A kilometre passed, then another, then five, then ten. My newfound companion was starting to look like she might be in for the long haul. Joe – a Yukoner and member of the support crew – drove past and quickly brought me up to speed on local laws. Apparently if a dog follows you for more than five kilometres, then it's 'your dog'.

To be honest I was really loving the company – they do say dogs are the best people. We chatted about life on the trail, shared some beef noodles, even a bit of beef jerky (although the noodles turned out to be far more popular). But as the hours passed, the kilometres started to pile up (23km from Fort Mc) and the sun started to disappear, I reminded myself that while enjoyable for me this was still someone's pet, there might even be some young kids at home wondering where there best four-legged friend had gone. As one of the support crew vehicles drove past I flagged them down and sadly asked them to give my new canine friend a ride back.

That left me back in the business of slowly but surely clocking up the kilometres. This ice road was essentially brand new – turned out it had been ploughed almost exclusively for us. The locals didn't mind and made good use of it, but until 48 hours ago it simply been non-existent. The first 8km were rough ice and snow, making it tough going, after that the ice smoothed out and you could hold a solid pace. I had chosen against putting ice spikes on my shoes, it stiffened up the sole and the straps could often cause rubbing on the feet. I also found it much harder to push the pace – instead I stuck with my trusty Hokas and simply made sure to carefully pick my line on the ice – avoid the really slippery stuff and try to keep some snow underfoot – just enough traction to stay balanced and propel yourself forward on each and every step.

The pink hues of dusk once again painted the horizon and eventually the sun disappeared leaving a cold, stark and starry night in its wake. Well into the night I decided to try and once again make up for the lost sleep from the last CP as well as grab some of the sleep I had actually planned for on this stage. I decided a decent two-hour break would be the call, walked until I found somewhat of a culvert on the side of the ice road (there was still some traffic from the locals, even in the early hours) and actually pitched my small one-person RAB tent and popped my bivvy inside. It cost only a few extra minutes to pitch the tent but the extra space and protection inside was a much welcome respite from the usual claustrophobic confines of the bivvy. Shoes off, jumped into the sleeping bag, set my alarm and drifted off.

Sometime later, I'm not exactly sure when, I awoke to sound of movement outside my tent. This was concerning on a whole lot of levels. Was it wildlife? If so, what? Was it a human? What were they doing? And more to the point what the hell was I going to do about it? I strained to listen and heard what I thought was my trekking poles being moved. My heart was starting to pound – I decided that if I heard the zips of my sled bag open I would have to get up and deal with whatever, whoever, was out there. Then suddenly, I heard no more. The crunch of receding footsteps, a car door and a casual vehicular departure. Leaving me wide awake and none the wiser as to what had just happened. Either way, seemed like a good time to pack up and move on!

I sorted and packed my bivvy up in the tent and stepped outside to be met by another spectacular light show courtesy of the northern lights. The scientist in me understands perfectly well what is going on up there in the ionosphere, but despite that you simply cannot help but be moved and left in awe of the sheer magnitude of those vast, delicate and alive dances of green light stretching from horizon to horizon. As it turned out my late-night visitor was the course photographer, Weronika. She had stumbled across my little camp under this cosmic display and had used some creative licence to relocate my trekking poles and safety lights to ensure she grabbed what turned out to be a picture of jaw-dropping magnificence – my little RAB tent and sled, pitched on a wide curve of ice road under a stunning northern lights display. It was nothing short of beautiful and once I had seen the picture she was instantly forgiven for scaring the life out of me.

The rest of this section was comparatively uneventful. Just long sweeping bends of the Peel River over and over until finally, on the right hand side of a sweeping left bend I sighted the trailer that was CP 4 - **Mid Peel River**. It was 6pm Sunday evening (over the preceding two days we had lost two hours – one due to changing states from the Yukon to the Northwest Territories – and one for the start of daylight savings). So while I had technically been racing for three days, five hours and change, the clock penalised us all an extra two hours. In reality – none of this mattered to me, I had arrived and it was time to simultaneously feel relieved to be able to stop but also to start the planning for how soon I could be moving again – on the long section to Aklavik. But another 45km north along the Peel river and the Arctic was slamming our 'summer weather window' shut.

CHAPTER 15

Aklavik

Mid Peel River (CP4) to Aklavik (CP5)

Section distance: 82km

Section time: 24 hrs 35 mins

Time at CP: 9 hrs 13mins

Total distance: 339km

Total time: 110 hrs 19mins

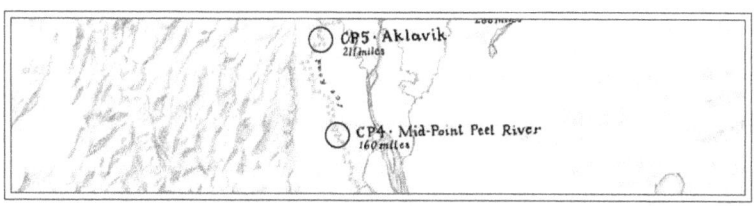

THE MID PEEL RIVER CHECKPOINT was nothing more than a leaky 8m metal trailer perched on the side of a frozen river. Stark, utilitarian and moderately fit for purpose. Despite all that, it was a welcome sight. I had been desperate to set eyes on it every turn and sweeping bend I dragged my sled around. There really is a mental and emotional juxtaposition when you get to a checkpoint like this. On one hand you have just completed what anyone else on any other day would consider to be a substantial ultra-marathon. Time for a well-earned rest and a few days recovery. But you haven't just completed an ultra-marathon – you've just completed over six marathons back to back and you've got a lot more to go. So the well-earned rest and few days' recovery suddenly vanishes and your 'rest' is actually filled with mundane administrative tasks like filling your thermoses and CamelBak, prepping a freeze-dried meal, reloading your wide-mouth flasks with trail mix and dry noodles ready for a fast prep on the trail in the coming dark hours ahead. This was the discipline, the training – the ability for my body and mind to accept that such a short break, after such a long stint, was sufficient to leave me ready to head out on an even longer section. There could be no deep recovery, no restorative sleep, only strategic decisions, the will to flip over a new mental page and strike out.

I took the time to have a mug of steaming black coffee and a freeze-dried meal of 'Himalayan Lentils & Rice'. The plan was to head out relatively quickly – try to get as much of the remaining daylight hours as possible, push as deep into the dark as I could and then sleep. This would be my fourth night out in a row and they were beginning to take their toll, both mentally and physically. I was keen to minimise their impact any way I could.

While I was eating, Avram reached the checkpoint. We had been swapping positions since the early hours of this morning but I had finally made a break and was keen to press on. Avram was his usual affable and happy self but seemed content not to push his pace – he repeatedly reiterated the danger of pushing too hard too early.

I headed out into the last few hours of sunlight – I managed to push just shy of 30km into this section before fatigue and the never-ending dark demanded that their toll be paid. The 30km took me a little over six hours – I decided to try and get around ninety minutes of sleep – an amount that seemed reasonable at the time but would appear luxurious and almost indulgent compared to what I would subject my body to in the final days of racing that lay ahead. It was cold and the thin layers of closed-cell foam between me and the thick layer of ice provided little comfort. Even in the best sleeping bag I could find, the layers of down could only hold back the relentless fingers of penetrating cold for so long. I packed up – an almost automated behaviour now – and set off, lasting another 12km before once again making the relatively strategic decision to sleep – you just reach a point where your progress is so painstakingly slow, there is no point fighting the inevitable. Grab as brief a sleep as possible that will allow a return to your planned pace once more. I grabbed thirty minutes, as verified by my trusty iPhone alarm clock and pushed on. Again.

Those early hours somewhere between 3am and sunrise (which was getting later and later the further north we travelled) were becoming a veritable minefield, it was like jungle warfare where your enemy was bone-crushing fatigue, lying in wait to ambush you at any moment. Sometimes it was a slow hunt, my pace began dropping, the legs heavy and footsteps less sure. The shoulders drop and the body would sway, eyelids impossibly heavy, the mind beset by a fog, heavy and dense. Suddenly I would snap awake – aware of what was happening – and try to push through. I would grab some trail mix from the wide-mouth bottle swinging on my hip, sing, talk, yell out, knowing I was only buying time against the inevitable. Other times it was a sudden and overwhelming assault. I was fine and then I was standing still, eyes closed, a slowly swaying statue on the ice. For me it seemed the only saviour was the sun. The scientist in me knew that the daylight was triggering all manner of biochemical processes that would stave off the exhaustion for just that little bit longer; the emotional human just wanted to see the sun and know that another night was behind me, not conquered, not vanquished, simply survived. In the morning daylight hours I managed a final thirty minute nap before the last stretch into Aklavik.

I packed up and struck out again – only to come across something wholly unexpected. I remember the sight vividly as it sparked a cascade of thoughts and emotions within me in an instant. It would be the beginning of a chain of events over the coming 36 hours that would alter my race entirely.

On the surface it sounds innocuous – I simply came across another competitor bivvying on the side of the trail. But who this was and what that meant was incredible. At first I didn't recognise what I was looking at – all but one competitor in the race had a sled that looked fairly similar. There were some alternatives but in general they were just variations on a theme – the ubiquitous high density polyethylene sled base in regulation blue, with either a single or dual axle wheelbase, fixed hauling arms and harness. That was all competitors bar one – David Hirschfield. David was rocking a $30 Amazon special – a three wheel enclosed running pram. On the surface it had some clear advantages, plenty of room to store your gear, a push not a pull system of propulsion, even gave you something to lean on when you needed a break. It also had a few drawbacks – by David's own admission – a brake system would have been nice on the long uphill sections.

All that aside – his 'Amazon special' was what I was coming across now in the early hours. The dawn light (and tiredness) made it difficult to clearly see until I was virtually right on it and the realisation came to hand. This was David, having a bivvy on the side of the trail. More importantly – this was one of the three current front runners. Someone who until about one minute ago was evidently in third place – only now he was in fourth and I was suddenly, technically in third place and albeit prematurely looking at a spot on the podium. That thought was immediately followed by the small voice that pointed out we still had approximately 270km to race – almost half the race to go – so perhaps we could 'calm the farm' and just focus on what needed to be focused on. Execute your plan, hold your pace and get to the next checkpoint. One checkpoint at a time – that was a strict policy. There was roughly a million things that could go wrong between now and the shores of the Arctic Ocean – a lapse of concentration and suddenly you have frostbite, a poorly adjusted balaclava and a stiff wind and you can wave your race goodbye due to some seemingly innocuous patch of frozen and dying flesh on your cheek. Mentally it was exciting to ponder the thought of somehow sneaking a toe hold onto the podium but the thought was quickly shelved.

With the rising sun and approximately 28km to go to Aklavik, the Arctic showed its teeth and reminded us why this vast and beautiful expanse was virtually uninhabited. Since encountering his bivvy, David and I had swapped positions a few times and now were travelling together – neither of us needed (or wanted) to 'run' into the checkpoint – and the plummeting temperature and hammering winds guaranteed that even if we wanted to, such behaviour was definitely not on the cards.

Heading into Aklavik I was well and truly wrapped up. I was wearing five layers – two thin thermal base layers, a light, medium and then heavy down jacket – face mask, full goggles, an additional thermal buff around my neck to block out any chance of snow and wind billowing anywhere unwanted, mid weight gloves and heavy duty mitts to finish off. I was sealed up and leaning hard into the wind as we ground down the last kilometres to the checkpoint. Similar to Fort McPherson, the final stretch into Aklavik seemed to be a never ending trail, sweeping and looping on and on with no apparent end in sight. The 'Welcome to Aklavik' sign seemed to have been erected far too prematurely from our perspective.

That last stretch was a low point both physically and emotionally for me. In Inuit, Aklavik means 'barren ground grizzly place' and while the grizzlies certainly weren't about, it was definitely living up to the 'barren ground' part. It was bleak, windswept and weather beaten. The katabatic-charged cold was penetrating and unrelenting. David seemed in reasonable spirits but this was one of the weakest moments for me from the standpoint of staying strong mentally. The township just seemed to never show up as we trudged on and on.

Eventually we spotted Neil Kapoor (a fellow returnee from 2017 who had withdrawn earlier in the race) who had very kindly walked out to meet us and bring us in so we didn't miss the turn. This wasn't just a kind act (which we both deeply appreciated) it was a display of some fortitude – the checkpoint was warm and sheltered and he was forgoing that for some time to finds us and walk us in. When he reached us and delivered the body blow message that we were still a several kilometres from the hall, I was gutted. I just needed a recharge out of the elements, a moment to regroup and shake off a long and unforgiving last 160km. I remember Neil asking if I was ok and repeatedly telling him, 'I just need to get into the checkpoint, I just need to get in.'

It had taken me 24 hours to get from CP4 at Mid Peel River to CP5 at Aklavik. What I didn't know at the time was that I had been the fastest competitor to cover that distance by a healthy margin. Unwittingly I had made up hours on the front runners – Patrick and Didier who were in front of me – and that was all about to change as I walked in the door.

CHAPTER 16
Inuvik

Aklavik (CP5) to Inuvik (CP6)
Section distance: 121km
Section time: 35 hrs 10 mins
Time at CP: 5 hrs 10 mins
Total distance: 460km
Total time: 150 hrs 39 mins

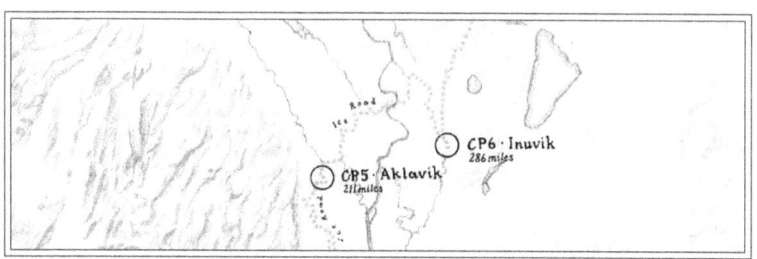

THE CHECKPOINT IN AKLAVIK was a small community hall – and I am convinced it was designed with the express purpose of confusing the daylights out of exhausted athletes. Add to that the fact that it was absolutely packed with medics, support crew, withdrawn racers and active racers and it was a veritable mad house

– less than ideal for recovery before heading out onto the longest single stretch between checkpoints of the entire race.

The downstairs section consisted of a basement/utility room – low ceilings, exposed pipes at perfect head height and loud water pumps and heating units, plus a main common room – a few couches and chairs buried in a sea of rolled out sleeping mats and bags. Upstairs was a tiny kitchenette, toilets and showers (no hot water) and believe it or not – an indoor swimming pool – empty of course.

My original plan was to get off my feet for a bit, eat some food and grab a decent sleep, hopefully a good few hours. The next section was long (120km), exposed and cold, so staying here before tackling it would be sensible and crucial.

Of sudden and singular importance to me, this was also the first time since the start line that I found myself in the same place as all the front runners. David and I had come in together, Patrick was upstairs trying to sleep in the empty pool facility (which was ridiculously cold, even by our significantly lowered standards), and Didier had been in for a while and was planning on heading out again before the rest of us, presumably to get a strong lead. That fact that we were all in the same spot, despite that fact that Patrick and Didier had been here for a few hours already – had a deep impact on me psychologically. I had started with no intentions of troubling the podium with my presence but now that the equation was starting to unfold and I could see the way through to making that a reality, my mindset changed.

Back in the cosy comfort of my heated office at home, pouring over spreadsheets and race results, I had noticed a clear and unsurprising trend – everyone who finishes the race has a much slower second half, in terms of pace (kilometres per hour) – almost without exception across a decade of results. Clearly this isn't earth-shattering, in fact you would've been surprised if it was otherwise. It was important because I had trained, planned and paced the preceding days on the ice with the purpose of producing what racers call a 'negative split'. In other words – the second half of your race is faster than your first.

For me this was somewhat of an insurance policy rather than some clandestine strategy – having enough in the tank to pull this off meant that you were strong going into the toughest stretch, when poor decisions, rough weather or just complete physical and emotional shutdown could knock you out of the race and write-off all your hard work in an instant. Now, potentially more importantly, it meant that having found myself up at the pointy end of the field, I had the physical and mental reserves to give myself options as to how I would attempt to play out the coming days and kilometres.

But back to the present – food and sleep – those were the priorities – but you can't sleep until you know what time you want to head out, that determines how long you can sleep and therefore what horribly short amount of time you are setting your timer for, so its incessant warbling can wake you and remind you that there is still so much work to do. Outside the wind was still absolutely hammering in, it was ferocious – but I'd managed to get an ear on some inside weather information. Word on the street was that the winds would drop significantly in the early hours of the morning, but until then would continue raging away. I had planned to sleep upstairs as I had been told it was cooler and much quieter than the hectic downstairs common room. Turns out that was half right – it was certainly quiet but it was also freezing, literally. The common room was too hot and too noisy so it looked like the basement utility room was the way to go – I moved my bed roll in there plus some gear to sort and Patrick quickly followed, having given up freezing upstairs next to the vast empty pool. David found himself a spot and amongst the whirring pumps and heating units we made the best of it, grabbing a few hours of fitful sleep.

I didn't know it at the time but the decisions and actions taken by the lead four athletes – David, Patrick, Didier and me – over the next 24 hours would shape the entire race. Patrick, David and I all decided to bunker down here at Aklavik until the very early hours of the morning, allowing the winds to hopefully drop off a little before we headed out, as well as giving our battered bodies some miniscule amount of respite.

Didier headed out hours before us, around 9pm – I assumed his plan was to strike out and get some distance on us, but the weather took its toll. According to checkpoint rumour mill he only managed a few kilometres before having to bivvy up and ride out the winds, basically mirroring our actions except he was trying to sleep in a wind-battered bivvy bag on the ice while we were attempting the same indoors in a utility services basement.

David, Patrick and I were all up around the same time with the plan of heading out together. David got sorted a little quicker than us and was keen to go – heading out before Patrick and I and getting some distance. Patrick and I headed out together around 2am into the inky blackness and still stiff winds. From the community centre it was a somewhat confusing meander down to the Peel River ice road again, from here we would stay on the river and through winding bend after winding bend work our way to Inuvik, some 120km away. Mentally for me Inuvik was a beacon, a shining light, for several reasons. First, I had long held the notion that mentally if I could get in and more importantly, out of Inuvik, then I could finish the race – yes it was still 160km to the finish line from there but it was simply about grinding it out, and once I was that 'close' I was sure nothing could stop me. Secondly the Inuvik checkpoint was at the Arctic Chalets, small huts that had the almost incomprehensible luxuries of a hot shower and soft bed. Incredible respite after around 450km of racing but a double-edged sword – all too easy to drop your guard and settle into its comforts for far too long. I wanted to get there but knew it would take discipline to stay the course and not dawdle in its creature comforts. It was the Hotel California of checkpoints.

Some days you're the hammer and some days you're the nail and for the first forty minutes or so out of the checkpoint I was very busy being the nail. I just couldn't get my act together – goggles kept fogging up, the buffs protecting my face kept freezing up and falling down, layers wouldn't sit right – and after being organised and on point for four days it was maddeningly frustrating as I seemed to have become stunningly incompetent. The stiff winds would find any minute gap around my goggles to sneak in and assault my eyeballs, or allow the fresh air and body heat trapped to fog up the lens and leave me completely unable to see.

If things aren't working – stop and fix it, because trudging on and complaining about it solves absolutely nothing. I told Patrick that I was a mess and was going to stop and get my act together, it would probably take twenty minutes and he should head on without me,

I would catch up with him as soon as I was sorted. It was freezing cold but it was time to play my favourite game – find the problem, fix the problem. I stripped off all the layers covering my head and reorganised the lot, digging into my sled bag to get some fresh buffs and balaclavas. Cleared my goggles, sorted out where the frigid air was creeping in and sorted that. Got all my layers back on and was ready to roll when my body decided that now was an ideal time for an urgent toilet stop – of the major kind, not the minor kind. It was about this time that I remembered I had put on a pair of insulated overpants when I left Aklavik to combat the cold – which seemed like a wise decision at the time – except that they were held up by braces, that had to be completely undone for me to drop trousers and deal with the immediate problem. In my haste I snapped the buckle on the right brace meaning I now had a very fiddly pair of overpants that on occasion decided to not remain on my hips but to check out what my feet were doing. Another problem to sort out before getting moving again – a few minutes of some hasty knots and jerry-rigging of the braces and we're sorted. Again.

All in all, I spent twenty minutes getting myself back into a state of organisation and back on the move. Best case, I thought Patrick would have picked up one and half kilometres on me – something I could make up comfortably – or so I thought.

I charged on, with my kit sorted and my pants hitched up and found a solid rhythm and strode on towards the dawn – certain that within maybe two hours I could rein Patrick in, leaving only David and Didier in front of us. The long sweeping bends left and right of the Peel River played out before me, over and over and over but no sign of Patrick. The horizon began to lighten, imperceptibly at first, then pink, then the sun broke past the low line of stunted trees that line the riverbank. Still no sign of Patrick – how far ahead was he? I pushed the pace a little more, determined now more than ever to run him down. Hours passed and passed and just when I thought I was going mad – I saw Patrick – and discovered why he had been so hard to catch, and that he wasn't alone, not by a long shot.

Turns out after leaving my disorganised self behind, he had hit the accelerator and kept it there, eventually running down not only David but the race leader Didier as well. Now all three of them were walking casually in a line stretching across the ice. My heart leapt – this wasn't just Patrick, this was the entire lead bunch, third, second and first all in a line. I picked up the pace once more and with a smile I inserted myself right in the middle of them.

'Howdy gents,' (insert cheeky grin) I said.

Patrick took a good look at me and replied, 'Well shit it's a race now isn't it?'

That comment was literal jet fuel for me. Ever since catching up with David I had quietly entertained the thought that maybe, just maybe, I could somehow creep a toe onto the podium, just third place, but imagine – a podium finish. Now, here was the entire podium laid out before me, with well over 200km to play out. All of a sudden it was anyone's game – and that lit a serious fire in the belly. It wasn't that I suddenly thought – this is it I can win, it was that I had the chance to throw down and give it everything I had knowing that the prize was some podium space. And who knew how high that space would be?

For the time being though it was back to reality and the ever-disciplined, well-trained athlete in my head told me to settle the hell down and focus on what was happening around me. For some random reason, most likely delirium, I had a mental flashback to a scene in Rocky Three when Clubber Lang's coach yells at him – 'You're the champ, you don't have to knock him out with one punch!' In other words, take a moment and play the smart game – there was still a tremendous amount of what would be brutal ground to cover before the dust would settle on this race.

Before I had joined them, 'the boys' as I referred to them, had all decided to move together at a slightly more comfortable but reasonable speed – no one was going to suddenly break and win from here. It was a smart move and I joined the club. While we were all competitive athletes, we were also a group of unique, interesting and socially adept humans, enjoying an incredible 'once in a lifetime experience' – with the obviously glaring incongruousness that three out of the four us were racing this event for the second time. The banter was relaxed as we talked about all manner of things, helping pass the time and the kilometres.

At one point, the suggestion was raised – in what I believe was part jest, part seriousness – that we could hold this pace, stick together and finish the race as a unit, joint first across the board. On the surface it was tempting, we could all hold a pace that would leave us well in front of the athletes behind us, the companionship was always welcome and these were three men I would be honoured to spend the next few days on the trails with. But after some thought the real answer became clear to me – I couldn't do it, because of my two young boys. Deep down I knew that I would rather have them see me take the risk, leave it all out on the field and lose – than take joint first place because of a deal, no matter how amicable.

I'm sorry guys, I'm calling every man for himself and I'll take the risk of the chips falling wherever they may. In the end it was Didier who verbalised what I was thinking – after a few hours of walking together he suggested everyone do what is right for them, rest, pace, stick together, drift apart. Do your thing. It was delivered not as an aggressive or assertive statement, simply a collegial observation – we all still had our own race to run – replete with our own demons, decisions and turning points.

Once that was out in the open I shocked the lot of them by announcing I was going to bivvy for a sleep. David looked at me with a quizzical expression,

'You know, that's the smart move, the exact right thing to do,' he said, 'Gutsy, but smart – and I bet none of us do the same.'

He was right. I took a solid 40-minute break and they charged on ahead for every single one of those minutes. I took the break with a peaceful mind though – I knew it was the right move, I knew deep down that I had plenty in the tank to draw on to run them down again. I knew it was going to be a long hard haul into Inuvik and we would all need to rest and sleep sooner or later – it was inevitable. No one, no matter how badly they wanted it, was going to make some miraculous, sleepless run for the next three days and clinch the win. This was still a long game. I was tired so as per my race plan, I took the rest. Simple as that. Forty minutes sounds like a miniscule amount of sleep given how long we had been on our feet and how little real sleep any of us had managed to grab. But it was the right move strategically. I knew it would be enough to recharge somewhat, get me back on my feet and would buy me another 8 to 12 hours of hard graft – exactly what I wanted.

My alarm sounded after forty minutes and literally ninety seconds later I was up, bivvy rolled and packed, and settling into my harness ready to set off. Mentally I felt strong, the knowledge that the entire lead pack was within a few kilometres and that I was part of it had reinvigorated me, a fire had been lit and stoked. I knew I had enough to finish the race, that was no longer a concern, now it was simply a matter of how hard could I push, what was I truly capable of? The thought sent a shiver down my spine – this was the exact reason – the exact reason I subject myself to these races and expeditions – to put myself in a position to see what I am truly capable of when we dig to the very bottom of the well, and then keep digging. What do we find when all is laid bare?

I knew it would take time to catch the boys and that it would require a solid and unrelenting pace. Food was consumed on the move, fluids drunk on the move, there was no five minute rest break here and there, I stuck with the policy I had had from the start – if you're not moving you're not finishing. Waste no time, be unflinchingly efficient in everything. I settled in and watched the afternoon fade into dusk and eventually dusk give way to full-blown night. Once again the northern lights graced us all with the elegant and majestic presence. I'm somewhat ashamed to admit that I doubt I gave them the time and admiration they deserved from this point on – I was focused, absolutely determined to push and run this pack down.

The light covering of snow on the ice gave me an almost pristine diary of what the trio ahead were doing. I could see the tracks of their sleds, the marks of their steps, regular as heartbeats metered out in the crisp white dialogue at my feet. What I didn't see were the telltale signs of a rest break or stop, the giveaway of mingled footsteps and deviation from the straight lines of sled wheel tracks. They had pushed, ever onwards with no apparent breaks either. From what I could see it looked like the race was well and truly on.

It was the very early hours of the morning – that dreaded time when the darkness is thick and almost inviting, your body and mind desperate for real sleep – that I finally saw them. Not moving, not talking, but three static sleds and three bivvy bags set out on the very side of the snowbank. I moved carefully and quietly until I was in line with them. Not to try and sneak past, the crunch of the snow and ice underfoot and under the wheels of the sled made that nigh impossible – but out of respect. There was no sound so I assumed they were fast asleep. I wouldn't want to be woken if I was asleep.

This was a pivotal moment; I remember it vividly. Once I walked past these three bivvies I would officially take the lead. Not as part of a group or spread out swapping back and forth. I would be clearly in front – and on top of that, everyone watching our GPS trackers back home, literally everywhere, would know that I had made a move into the lead and would be watching to see what happened next. There would be no respite from here – from this point on they would be chasing. I would not know how close or far they were, what state they were in, if asleep or on the move. It would be me and me alone, executing the remainder of the race as best I could in a bid to not just land on the podium but to climb its heights.

'This is it.

'Take it and do not look back.

'They do not pass.'

Spoken aloud. To myself. A deal struck. A promise made. It was galvanising.

The euphoria and excitement of the moment was, to some degree, short lived – there was still literally days of racing until the finish line would be in sight. Now the execution of my race strategy was crucial, every decision seemed heavier, measured against the risk of falling back and the desire to extend the lead. The delicate balance between smart decision-making and brave risk taking.

To that end, I pushed ahead for another forty minutes and decided to grab a twenty-minute power nap. Just enough to keep me on my feet with pace until the sun came up but not enough that the chasers would overrun me – even if they had suddenly hopped up and charged down the trail after me. As it turns out they did no such thing – for while I was 'indulging' in those brief moments of sleep – all hell was breaking loose only a few kilometres behind me. The next five hours would see the drastic withdrawal of one of the chase pack, the destruction of a sled and a significant amount of gear not to mention the intervention of Royal Canadian Mounted Police, aka 'the Mounties'

'He needs help.'

Here is my understanding of what was occurring just a few kilometres behind me during those fateful early morning hours. I was not there, this is based on later discussions and images.

At some point Didier realised he was in trouble – whether due to single prolonged exposure or a cumulative episode – hypothermia appeared to have taken a grasp on him. He found himself unable to get warm, apparently somewhat delirious, and called on Patrick and David for help.

Both men acted – put their race plans aside and immediately set to work trying to warm Didier. Body heat, sleeping bags appeared to be of no avail. Didier was becoming increasingly erratic, trying to run away and being uncooperative with their attempts to settle and warm him. At some point, the decision was made to press the emergency help button on Didier's GPS SPOT device.

(*A quick primer on SPOT devices – the ones used for the 6633 served multiple purposes. They are a small orange box roughly the size of a pack of cigarettes, attached to your sled by the race crew just before the race starts. Its first function is to serve as a GPS tracker – allowing both the race crew and anyone watching via the internet at home to see where you are on the course and giving some basic data about speed, distance to and from nearby checkpoints. The second function was as a rescue device. The unit had two buttons on it – the left button alerted the race director that you needed help, the right hand button was the 'send everyone' button for when an athlete was in extreme danger, it alerted the race director and local emergency services simultaneously. Pressing either button meant instant disqualification but ensured that immediate help was on its way.*)

Unfortunately, the button while pressed gives no indication as to whether the alert message has been successfully sent, let alone received at the other end. The three athletes had no way of knowing if the support crew and medics were on their way, how far away they were, or if they were coming at all.

As Didier's condition deteriorated they became concerned over his breathing, whether laboured or just shallow I do not know. It would no doubt have been complicated by the level of exhaustion of both Didier and those helping him. He may have simply been drifting in and out of an exhausted state of slumber. Either way the decision was made to take what could be considered extreme measures to warm him. They gathered whatever seemed flammable and piled it on top of Didier's sled and bag and set it alight in a bid to make a small fire to generate some heat. Keep in mind that the Arctic is not conducive to plant growth – and coming out of winter, what little tree coverage there is is not only a long way behind the banks of the ice road, it is also heavily stunted and burdened with a dense layer of snow. There was no way they could collect any type of flammable material outside of what they had on their persons, not without hours of hard graft – time they felt that they did not have. The one flaw in this plan was the small canister of winter mix fuel within Didier's supplies – a piece of mandatory gear allowing an athlete to fire up a small stove for the purposes of water, food or simply heat. The small fire was eventually enough to cause the canister to explode – thankfully leaving all three men unscathed but immolating Didier's sled and redistributing much of its now charred contents across the frozen Peel River.

Not knowing if help from the race crew was on the way, they decided to press the right-hand help button on the SPOT to send out a call for help direct to the police and emergency services. If the system worked then there would be no doubt that help was on its way and it would most likely be substantial in response and capacity. The three men waited.

While this had been happening, several kilometres away I had wrapped up my nap, swiftly packed and was once again pushing ahead in the blackness of night. Suddenly I could make out headlights coming towards me. Given the time of night, in such a remote area, a random local car was highly unlikely – I was not surprised to see one of the support crew vehicles pull up beside me. What they asked and told me however was surprising.

'Do you know where Didier and the other guys are?'

'Yeah I'd guess they are about three to four kilometres back on the left of the trail.'

'They've hit the emergency button – gotta go.'

Definitely not what I expected – my first, and really only thought, was that I hoped they were all ok. For any one of those three to hit the SPOT button, knowingly and immediately ending their race, would not have been an action taken lightly.

Not long after that encounter another vehicle, this time the RCMP (Royal Canadian Mounted Police).

'You ok?'

'Yep.'

'Then it sounds like we are looking for the next athletes.'

'About three to four kilometres further along is my best guess.'

There was nothing I could do to assist and no point dwelling on what 'might' be going on. I had to continue to operate under the assumption that the three of them were ok and that potentially two of them were still racing. So I pushed on. After an hour or so, both the support vehicle and RCMP vehicle came back past me heading towards Inuvik – I believe Didier was in with the RCMP. As the race support vehicle came past I could see Patrick and David inside. Now I was really confused. Had all three athletes just withdrawn? Were they all injured? The most plausible explanation was hypothermia but all three at once? I pushed on, focus on your own race.

To add even further to the confusion, sometime later the support vehicle came back past me again with Patrick and David inside. Now I officially have no idea what was happening but by the looks of it, Didier was out of action and Patrick and David were back. Are they ok? Are they injured but didn't want to withdraw? Did they go just to support Didier? No idea. Focus on your own race. Push on.

The sun rose and Inuvik pulled the same damn trick that every township had so far – just when you think you are close, someone tells you that, 'Yes you're very close, only about ten miles [16km] to go'. When your pace is around 6km per hour, learning that you are 'only' 16km out is nothing short of soul crushing.

Ten miles. Sixteen kilometres, that sounds even worse. That's when from somewhere in my training I remembered the piece by Jocko Willink .

What do you do when you have a task that you really don't want to do? When it's mundane, boring, demoralising, crushing?

Simple. You do it harder.

Give no quarter and crush it.

So first of all make peace with the fact that those 16km are getting done – one way or another. So you may as well hit them as hard as you can and get them over and done with. Standing here having a pity party for one is covering exactly zero meters.

So I hit it.

I power walked like a man possessed, the occasional jog to see what that felt like (terrible), but just crush the distance. I made the last swing to the right that left me with the long straight final run into

Inuvik. I'd done this section in 2017 on a post-race jaunt onto the ice road – the only time at all in 2017 that I actually spent on the ice. I knew it was long, but I knew it ended – so less talk and more do.

For the final few kilometres some of the support crew came out to walk in with me. The sun was out and it was a glorious afternoon. While the crew weren't racing, they were still leading very hectic days and nights either in cars or checkpoints, so a few kilometres in the sun was no doubt very appealing for them.

A final turn off the ice road, a final climb and I had arrived at the Arctic Chalets. A guaranteed peaceful checkpoint – all withdrawn athletes were housed elsewhere with strict instructions not to disturb the remaining racers. There would be a real bed, a shower (maybe even a hot one) and a chance to get re-organised physically (the inside of my sled bag was a mess), mentally and emotionally. There was also a noticeable change in my interactions – I was now officially and clearly the race leader. First into Inuvik after the monstrous 120km section. The combination of the sunlight, being in the lead and being quietly proud of the way I had tackled the last 16km had left me in good spirits – and apparently it showed. Several of the crew commented that I looked far too fresh and composed for this deep into the race. This buoyed me even further.

The last strange moment came as Martin lead me towards the hut set aside for racing athletes. Out of nowhere a tall man stepped over introducing himself as the director of a German documentary/news team who happened to be in town. As I was the race leader, they were keen for an interview to discuss the race, would that be ok? It took me completely by surprise and while I wanted to be polite I was incredibly conscious of the race clock ticking away. In a split second decision I offered to hopefully catch them further up the trail, explained that I was under a bit of time pressure and perhaps they would like to chat to Martin. Flattering as it was, I thought that would be the last I would see of them – turns out I was wrong.

CHAPTER 17
Gateway

Inuvik (CP6) to Gateway (CP7)
Section distance: 68km
Section time: 21 hrs 30 mins
Time at CP: 56 mins
Total distance: 488km
Total time: 173 hrs 25 mins

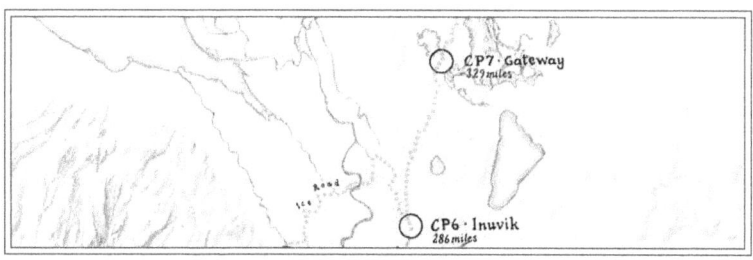

THE CABIN THAT WAS SET ASIDE for racers was also shared with the medic and the support crew. It looked like it slept maybe four in very close quarters but was now crammed full with medics Jonny and Scott, race director Martin and support crew personnel Evan, Mimi, Richard and Emily. Not to mention Didier who had been quickly discharged from hospital and was recovering in the same cabin.

A short steep set of stairs lead to the living area – a tiny kitchenette, a bedroom with a double and single bed at one end and a living/lounge space at the other end. Scotty pulled me aside for a quick medical check over – extremities checked for signs of frostbite or cold injury, feet checked for blisters or other issues. I was in surprisingly good shape, hands and fingers fine, feet in relatively good shape. I had some blisters and fairly painful shin splints – but given the distance and pace nothing unexpected.

I got a freeze-dried meal heated up so I could eat while I got my sled bag opened and sorted out. It had been everything from closet, kitchen, bin and office since Fort McPherson some three hundred kilometres ago – the last time I had a space indoors to sort my kit. So I ate, cleaned, restocked and reorganised. Next on the list was a shower – an almost unbelievable luxury. Thankfully the freezing cold meant not only that you don't sweat significantly but also that your nasal passages and sinuses were completely frozen, which equates to pretty much no sense of smell, so I had no idea how 'fresh' or otherwise I actually was. I was more concerned about a far more painful and shall we say 'sensitive' issue – chafing.

The degree of chafing between my upper thighs and buttocks was nothing short of biblical. This is a common problem on ultras and can literally spell the end of your race if not handled properly. I knew it would be an issue and had come well prepared with a superb anti-chafing cream that is often used by bike riders.

That sounds all well and good but of course the Arctic always throws you an added degree of difficulty – a tub of anti-chafe cream is fine until you realise that within an hour of starting the race you now have a tub of cream that has frozen into a solid ball. Useless. I had learnt from bitter experience and was well prepared for that too – way back in Whitehorse in the comfort of my hotel room, I had gone through the messy process of dividing the cream up into a small resealable sandwich bags so I could keep one tucked into my race-vest pocket, close to my skin, keeping it warm and therefore not frozen. I had been applying this cream liberally almost every six hours but the chafing was still incredible. This shower was going to hurt.

Before jumping into the shower I realised that I was also missing two other items – I had no soap, shower gel or deodorant. Hell I only had one pair of underwear – in a bid to keep the weight of my supplies down to the absolute minimum every conceivable 'creature comfort' or luxury (like a spare pair of jocks) had been well and truly dropped off the packing list.

A sheepish request and thirty seconds later I had Richard's (race crew) shower gel (donated by his wife Mimi, in Richard's absence – thanks Richard!) and Jonny's (medic crew) deodorant. Perfect.

The shower was sensational. To clear off the dirt, grime, grit; to give the hair and beard a good scrub; to embrace the cleansing pain of giving the chafed areas a good clean – it was all magnificent. But that race clock in my mind was ticking away – no time to waste. The shower was magical but short lived.

Last task was a sleep – in a bed no less. Now the question – how long can I sleep for?

For the first half of the race this question had been purely utilitarian, how much sleep do I need to keep moving and hold my pace? Now it was purely strategic – how little can I get away with. Too little and I'll be unable to maintain pace and will only have to sleep again and again on the frozen, windswept trail ahead – no bed there. Too much and you let the chase pack make up valuable ground. In the end I settled on an indulgent three hours. More sleep than any single day since Thursday, almost a week ago. I set my timer and passed out within seconds.

I woke up before the timer went off. Not because I was rested and refreshed, not because I had been disturbed – I believe it was because literally every fibre of my being was in race mode. I had slept for about two and a half hours. I'd had enough and I needed to move. I got up, dressed and set about filling my thermoses ready to strike out once more.

How much of a lead did I have? I thought I might probe the support crew present to see what I could find out – that discussion gave me an answer, but it was one I really didn't want.

I had arrived at Inuvik at 14:15 on Wednesday, we had been racing now for over 145 hours straight. On arrival I was well over five hours ahead of the next competitors – David and Patrick – but that was about to be cut to virtually nothing.

Martin informed me in broad strokes of what had happened with Didier during the previous night, stating that they would be issuing both Patrick and David with individual time credits to essentially reinstate the time they had given up while helping Didier. For those who are not familiar with the ultra racing world – it often happens that a runner may get into some distress and need assistance and it is also not uncommon for other runners to take some time to assist them. But it's not common for those racers who assist to be given any time credit for their actions. They are thanked for being an upstanding member of the ultra-running community as well as a decent human being and left to continue their race.

A few things were different here – firstly the amount of time, it wasn't ten or fifteen minutes, it was a matter of hours. Secondly, the organisers had some capacity to measure that time with accuracy. They had to rely on Patrick and David giving an accurate 'start' time but they could definitely state a very clear finish time. I have no doubt that the start time given by both men would have been their honest best guess. So while the issuing of a time credit was unusual and the amount of credit given substantial, I could understand both. Clearly it would add a very significant degree of complexity to my race but so be it. Martin began going into the details of how they arrived at the figures and while I could have spent time assessing their process and logic, arguing points such as the fact that both competitors had been off their feet and warmed in a vehicle for a significant amount of time, I knew that both of them had acted honourably, there would be an emotional and mental toll from the episode that couldn't be measured and lastly, I didn't want to argue, it was what it was. I was determined to win. I cut Martin off.

'Just tell me the number. How much do I have to beat them by?' Martin delivered the news. 'You can't just win. You have to beat them by a healthy margin.'

'Just tell me the number.'

'Four hours and forty-seven minutes, you have to beat Patrick by at least four hours and forty-seven minutes.' Martin paused then continued, 'So if you cross the finish line first and Patrick crosses it four hours and forty-six minutes after you – he will win.'

My response was instant.

'Ok. I have to go.'

In my mind the process was simple. Just tell me the number and I will go out and deal with it. I had come into Inuvik with a five-hour and eighteen-minute lead. That lead was now a mere thirty-one minutes. Now, more than ever I was glad that I had stayed disciplined here in what would have been an ideal checkpoint to spend significant time.

I quickly arranged the last few items of my gear and headed down and out to once more set off into another night. Evan offered to walk me out through the township to ensure I found my way onto the right road out of town. The trail doubled back at first to retrace the last kilometre or so into Inuvik – and on my way out I came across David and Patrick coming in. I'm not ashamed to say that I saw that they looked beat, so I set the shoulders back, picked up the pace and put on a smile. Everything mattered from now on. Everything. So fight on all fronts, physical, mental, emotional. I didn't know if it made any difference but it couldn't hurt for them to see me already heading back out, in good spirits and shape before they had even arrived.

Moving on, Evan and I chatted as we walked the few kilometres though houses and streets to the outskirts of town until I found myself looking out over a long straight stretch of road.

'This is it,' he stated, 'just stay on this road until the end.'

And it literally was the end, stay on this road until you run out of road, run out of land, run out of Canada. Literally go until you are standing on the six-metre thick frozen shelf of ice that is the surface of the Arctic Ocean at this time of year. Go until the end.

What I didn't know then, but do now, is that I was the most efficient racer in and out of Inuvik. I spent a total of five hours and ten minutes – from walking in to walking out. The next quickest competitor spent more than seven hours. I departed Inuvik at 7:23pm Wednesday evening, Patrick and David wouldn't leave until 6:31am Thursday morning, both having spent almost four hours longer in the checkpoint than me. During the race, this type of information would have been monumental – but I had no such luxury. As the race leader you lose the knowledge of the position of those chasing you. They can see your time in and out of checkpoints as they come in after you – they can reasonably calculate how far ahead you might be, but I knew nothing. They could be hours behind, or minutes. I knew both of them had arrived into Inuvik as I left, but did they spend five hours there like me – or far less? Or much more? I had to assume that they were just behind the last hill. In my mind they were breathing down my neck. There could be no other way.

With Martin's words, 'four hours and forty-seven minutes,' ringing in my ears, I made my way on the final road to Tuk – all 160km of it. As I headed out of Inuvik, sled trailing behind me, a few returning locals in pickups stopped to ask where I was going. The answer of 'Tuk' was always met with a raised eyebrow and a chuckle, 'Good luck!'

The sun slowly set, once again casting amazing pink and red hues amongst the clouds. But with the disappearance of the sun came the cold. Bitter cold – far harsher than anything any of us had encountered all race. The temperature plummeted, bottoming out at -37C. Being out alone in that degree of cold is difficult to explain – I'm often asked what -30 and -40C feels like. The sun makes a difference during the day, seemingly taking the edge off of such extremes, but at night there is no respite. The temperature is like a malevolent force, a constant onslaught, like a thousand small knives all relentlessly driving home into your very bones. It just does not stop. Ever. Any exposed skin is assaulted constantly, running the risk of frostbite within minutes.

For the first time since the start line, I found myself battling not for pace or speed but literally for survival. Survival in tiny increments. I knew I had to act and play the next ten plus hours until the sun returned very, very carefully. My first step was to bivvy up for twenty minutes – partially for sleep but more to try and warm up. My shoes came off but I was in my sleeping bag (rated to -40C) wearing everything I had. I set the timer for twenty minutes and curled up into the smallest ball I could. I lasted the twenty minutes but was no warmer. Packing up the bivvy took less than two minutes but I was still shaking almost uncontrollably by the time I had my harness back on and was on the move.

Move and move fast. Get the heart rate up. Get the core warm. I zipped up every layer, grabbed the sides of my jacket hood and brought my forearms together vertically on my chest. I was sealed up as much as possible. The plan was simple – move for fifteen minutes. Stay strong mentally for fifteen minutes. Ignore the cold and the pain for fifteen minutes. And when that fifteen minutes is up…do it again…and do it again, and again. Just survive until the sun comes up.

I was on my second or third fifteen- minute stint when a vehicle pulled up beside me. It was Jonny and Scotty, the medics. Jonny lowered his window and gave me one of his trademark cheeky grins. 'How's it going?'

Before I tell you my reply – let me give you some context. Up until this point I had made a strict habit of three actions since the start of the race. Always wave at truck drivers, always stop to talk to support crew/medics/photographers and lastly – positive dialogue. If anyone asks, you feel great. Verbalise the positive – even if it's a stretch from the truth. The idea was simply to vocally reinforce a positive mindset. And up until that moment I had stuck to those three rules – time for one of them to break.

'Yeah, we're having a rough day.'

They knew it. That was why they were there. It was roughly 3am, around -37C and I was the only athlete out of the Inuvik checkpoint. Everyone else was either tucked up in a warm checkpoint or well behind and potentially in a 'warmer' spot.

'We just figured with the temperature, the dark, knowing that around this time your hormones would be somewhere in the bin and that your mind would be screaming for a sleep – we might come out a pay you a friendly visit.'

It was most welcome – and multi-purpose. For me it took my mind off the relentless onslaught of the cold and dark. For the medics they knew they were helping me out but they were also assessing – speech, alertness, motor skills, fingers, extremities. They were having a chat but simultaneously working through a mental checklist. We chatted for what felt like ten or so minutes. The warmth emanating from the car was heaven. Just enough to dull the fierce edge of the true temperature. It was enough to give me the strength to push on for a few more hours, literally begging the sun to come up.

Mentally, I knew this was going to be the second last night I had to face. It was my sixth in a row and they had taken their toll – those first few nights seemed like a mere training run compared to the brutality of these last two. And I was about to find that lurking hidden in the last few hours of both of these nights was a disaster that could potentially not only knock me off the podium, but end my race completely.

The first time it happened I had no idea what was going on. One minute I was holding pace when suddenly, I was no longer moving forward. I wasn't moving at all. Hell I wasn't even on my feet. In the space of split second – I had gone from moving to being face down on the road. The trail here was hard-packed, wind-scoured gravel and ice. Not exactly forgiving.

I got up as quickly as I could, not through any heroic measure to charge ahead, but more out of shock – *hope that it was nothing and move on*. I got going – and lasted about fifty paces.

Wham. Straight back down. Walking, blackout, face down on the ground. Only this time the pain made itself known as well. I had barely had enough reflex to stop my fall. Based on the pain I had slammed onto my kneecaps and then fallen forward. My right kneecap especially was very unhappy about the whole scenario.

Now I was worried. I was roughly thirty hours from the finish line. I was in first place, I had no idea how much, or how little, of a lead I had on Patrick and to a lesser extent, David. And now in the final stretch my body seemed to have decided to fail in a very serious way. I panicked. In my mind's eye I saw Patrick and

David catch and pass me as I struggle to make progress. What if this kept happening, what if my legs just gave out completely, what if I blacked out and didn't wake for hours? Everything I had fought for and sacrificed – not just in the last seven days but every day for the last twelve months of training – all of it could be about to disappear in an instant.

No.

Not on my watch.

You're smarter than that.

Find the problem, fix the problem.

First thing, get on your feet, lean hard on those poles and get moving. I called out every step aloud, focused on planting the foot and moving forward, 'one, two, three' – get to fifty and start again.

Next – work the problem. Potential explanations – hypoglycaemia, dehydration, extreme exhaustion, something more sinister.

Solve for X – step one, eat. If it's something to do with your blood sugar just bottoming out, you can fix that. I thought it was unlikely but would cover all bases. I grabbed the wide mouth bottle swinging off my waist harness and consumed about a third of the bottle of trail mix – I knew there was plenty of carbohydrates in there and about 400 calories.

Step two – are you dehydrated? Gross as it may seem I had been keeping an eye on my urine – colour and frequency since day one. It's not exciting but it's the quickest and easiest way to check if your fluid intake is up to scratch and that your kidneys are functioning. No pee or dark pee and 'Houston, we have a problem'. But no problems there. Strangely enough excessive urination is also an early warning sign of impending hypothermia – cold induced diuresis.

Thankfully no problems here so I ticked that one off the list.

Step three – extreme exhaustion. Ockham's Razor said this was the most likely answer – all things being equal, the simplest answer is usually the correct one. Those early hours of the morning I knew I'd been getting slower and slower, meandering and literally falling asleep on my feet. At one point I woke up and realised I had been walking along completely asleep – based on some rough calculations it looked like I had been walking, asleep, for almost six kilometres. I was simultaneously concerned and really impressed that I multi-tasked beautifully – got a snooze and keep something of a pace – and best of all, didn't end up face first in a snowbank, rudely awoken by the sudden snow bath.

Eat, drink, get a quick bivvy. At this point I was too scared to stop for more than twenty minutes – so a quick nap was all I could do. Stop, bivvy out, shoes off, into sleeping bag wearing everything. Twenty minutes later exactly, up, out, shoes on, roll up bivvy, harness on, go.

The sun finally broke through. The clouds looked like they were caught in a jet stream streaking out from the sun, giving the sky a strange, stretched appearance. It was so striking, I actually stopped and remembered to grab a few quick photos. As I was tucking my phone away a beaten old pick-up came towards me from the north and pulled up beside me. The driver had the weather-beaten look of a local – he leant over and asked me where I was going.

'Tuk.'

He thought for a moment before replying,

'It's blowin', I wouldn't be goin'.'

He chuckled, wished me luck and drove off.

Blowing a gale or not, I was going. Come hell or high water.

The sun was like a battery pack, my legs seemed to regain some strength, the exhaustion seemed to recede some way into the recesses of wherever it was hiding. Make hay – go, go, go. I knew there was still another checkpoint to reach at Gateway and another full night ahead. I knew the checkpoint would be spartan – just a windswept trailer so the respite would be brief – and the night terrified me. The thought of it being the last and that the coming day would see an end to it all was the only thought that let me stave off the fear.

This stretch of road was true wilderness. There was nothing but rolling hills and stark white for as far as you could see. It was simultaneously featureless and beautiful. I was regularly torn between head down race mode and stopping to look around and soak it all in. No matter what, cross that finish line and it would be over. I had no intentions of coming back (despite having said that multiple times on multiple continents and almost always coming back…)

If I was going to survive the coming night but also stave off the chasers behind me I had to find the fine balance between moving fast during the day but also getting enough strategic 'sleep' to allow me to keep moving as much possible. I made the call to take one longer break rather than several shorter ones. The theory being that it would be more restorative if I could get a deeper sleep cycle in, rather than a stopgap measure of something short. I bivvied up and set my alarm for ninety minutes. Purely strategic and best guess, based on the concept of the average sleep cycle being ninety minutes in length. I had no idea where Patrick or David were but I had a good feeling for what I needed to push hard – there was still the best part of 100km to go.

The final checkpoint – Gateway – a frozen, leaking trailer with its tail gate stuck wide open, finally came into view and I walked into it at 16:53 on Thursday afternoon. I had no idea at the time but here is what was happening timewise. Patrick and I had left Aklavik (CP6) together, based on our departure times from Inuvik (CP7), when Patrick and David left Inuvik I was nine hours ahead but then account for their time credit and that gave me a lead of just over four hours – primarily thanks to having pushed the pace hard all the way from Aklavik to Inuvik and partly because I was in and out of Inuvik four hours faster than them. But based on our respective arrival times into Gateway, the picture had changed dramatically – somewhere along the way Patrick had left David behind and cut my lead down to just four hours – *not* taking into account his time credit. I had got slow and he had got fast – apply his time credit and he was technically now in the lead – by an hour. Remember that out on the field I had no idea of this – Patrick would once he got to Gateway as he could see what time I had arrived and left, but I was completely in the dark.

How long we would each spend at Gateway would be crucial beyond belief. How long we would each need would depend on all manner of factors – how exhausted we each were, whether we would we sleep here, eat here, what our pace would be from here to the finish line. I would make a decision here that set us both up for a final showdown.

CHAPTER 18
Tuktoyaktuk

Gateway (CP7) to Tuktoyaktuk (Finish)
Section distance: 88km
Section time: 22 hrs 22 mins
Total distance: 596km
Total time: 195 hrs 47 mins

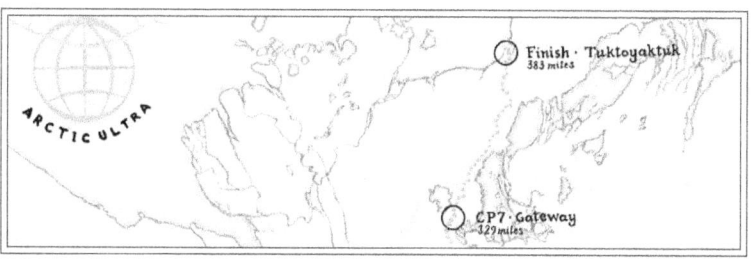

FOR THE MONTHS LEADING UP to the race I had been working on a spreadsheet – refining, tweaking, adjusting, testing. All for one purpose – to produce a small laminated card that would sit in my pocket for the course of the race. That little laminated card listed every checkpoint, the distances between, what pace I would do between each and how long I would spend at each, resting. It was a very brave, very carefully thought out, partially speculative, holy grail of race strategy for me. It even had a finish time – the time I would cross the finish line after racing 614km in, what at the time of creating the card, were completely unknown conditions. I had constructed those times based on analysis of all the finishers from the preceding years, especially 2018 when the new longer course had been introduced. It took into account the pacing I had done in training, what I had experienced in 2017, every piece of data I could get my hands on.

And that time-card told me one thing about Gateway aka CP7.

Get in and get out.

You have minutes here – not hours.

In the end I was in and out in 54 minutes. Albeit a very hectic and action-packed 54 minutes.

Patrick would stay there for just under three hours.

When we respectively left and the time credit was applied – I was back in the lead – by just under one hour.

Literally less than sixty minutes separated us.

We had been racing for almost 180 hours and the difference between first and second place was now mere minutes.

We had 88km to go.

We both would have to survive another night out.

And the gently undulating trail was over. The hills were back.

The Arctic was out for its last pound of flesh and its cold, dark hands would flay it from both of us.

But back to my action-packed 54 minutes at Gateway.

The trailer was parked on a small exposed rise. For reasons I'm still not sure of, the back of the trailer was wide open. It wasn't facing into the wind but it meant the temperature in the trailer was exactly the same as outside. You were somewhat out of the wind but that was it. To my surprise there was a well rugged up group of Germans waiting for me.

It was the news crew that had introduced themselves in Inuvik – I had politely declined the interview then and had in part jest/part seriousness suggested I could see them at the next checkpoint – knowing full well that CP7 would be lonely, freezing trailer in the middle of literally nowhere. And now – here they were.

'Can we grab that interview now?'

Absolutely, because I'm impressed – only one problem, I'm really conscious of time, so I made them a deal – I'm happy to answer any questions but while I'm doing that I will also be getting changed, eating food and getting my sled sorted for the final stretch. So in this 8m trailer, packed with bags, gas, stove burners for heating water, a few well-worn chairs, I hastily started getting changed, made up a freeze-dried meal of chocolate mud cake (serves two people – not today it doesn't!) and tried my best to provide coherent answers. I quickly stripped off layers in front of two cameramen, a sound guy and the lead interviewer. I still have no recollection of what they asked or what I gave in reply. One day I hope to find the interview to actually see what happened. I also secretly hope that I didn't hallucinate the entire thing – can't rule that out.

I managed to fill all my thermoses – which was becoming no mean feat, in this extreme cold even the support crew were having problems getting cooktops running long enough to boil water before the fuel lines froze. There is a reason no one lives out here – beautiful as it is, nature makes it very clear that you are welcome to pass through but you are most certainly not welcome to stay.

I left Gateway at 17:46 Thursday evening. The wind was picking up and the sun, along with the temperature, was once again preparing to plummet for the evening. The final evening. The one point of solace – no matter what happened tonight this would be the last night. Patrick would arrive at Gateway approximately three hours after I departed, and he would stay for almost three hours. That, combined with my fast entry and exit, gave me back the lead. Adjusted for his time credit, when Patrick left that checkpoint I had a lead of exactly sixty minutes. I have no idea if he knew this at the time, I know that I certainly didn't.

Why did he spend that time there? Why did I spend so little? I can only speculate but it's my belief that the difference was race strategy on the trail – Patrick had made up an enormous amount of ground on me from CP6 to CP7. I believe he managed that by having very little, if any sleep, on that section, relative to me. Which meant that at CP7 he had no realistic option other than to have a decent break and get some serious rest before setting off for the final chase home. Multiple short power naps were keeping me on my feet and moving – diminishing returns without a doubt, but the end was almost in sight so we probably both felt that now was the last chance to 'leave it all out on the field'. There would not be another section on which to catch up or make ground.

Eighty-eight kilometres, 55 miles. That's all there was. The entire outcome of the race, in podium terms, would be decided in those frozen miles. And so we raced.

I knew I couldn't make it one stint without some sleep along the way. Best guess was that I had a little over twenty hours of work in front of me – and it wouldn't be easy work. The road into Tuk was hilly, not 'undulating' as our race director described it. It was going to be hard climbs with very few corresponding descents. One of the finishing athletes from 2018 about this last section told me, 'That last thirty kilometres may as well be a hundred – it's rough.'

That was coming from someone whose resumé left no doubt that he was old-school hard material. If he said it was rough then it was probably closer to soul crushing for the rest of us. So for a fair portion of this section it would be strategy and for the last portion is would just be grit. Pure, unadulterated grit.

Four hours out of Gateway I grabbed an hour of sleep. More than I wanted to risk, less than I really needed. The sun vanished and the last night stole over the sky and descended to bear down upon us. Much of this night was almost dreamlike to me. In fact most of my knowledge about it is drawn from the data off of my watch – which was tracking via GPS my movement – and from post-race feedback from Patrick on what he saw in my tracks as he attempted to run me down. The trail itself wound left and right, over and over with what seemed like an endless parade of small yellow arrow signs on the side of the road indicating the direction of the monotonous sweeping bends.

Based on watch data, I would hold a strong pace then suddenly slow and stop, and usually between five and eight minutes later I would take off again. Best guess was that I had fallen asleep standing up and was literally and figuratively frozen on the spot. It looked like I managed to do that four or five times across the first fourteen hours from leaving Gateway. Patrick told me that he could watch my sled tracks go from straight, to meandering and then finally into sweeping circles as I literally walked around on the spot, probably asleep. He then asked me if I had started 'falling down' as he noticed several patterns in the snow that looked like I had collapsed on the spot. He was not wrong.

My arch-nemesis of blacking out and slamming into the ground returned once again during the inky depths of pre dawn. I would stop and make a hot drink, usually a carbohydrate-based refuel sports drink to try and keep the legs moving and brain functioning. I had long since moved past the point of coffee having any true stimulant value. The exhaustion and sleep deprivation was all encompassing that the coffee only served to push my heart rate up and do little else.

As these episodes returned I met them not with fear but rage. I knew what was happening, chemically my hypothalamus was completely overwhelmed and my cerebral-spinal fluid was completely awash with waste products and biochemicals that should have been flushed out during repeated restorative cycles of deep sleep – the exact sleep I had not been getting for the last seven nights. I was literally at war with myself as I tried to fight the laws of biochemistry through sheer force of will. I am not ashamed to admit that on both this morning and the previous, as I came to on the ground and pushed back to my feet, that tears streamed down my face as I felt my race slipping away from me – almost as though my body was betraying me in the final moments. (Despite what I had put it through over eight days – I was driven enough to question how it could dare not function as I demanded.) In the end I knew that all that mattered was staying on my feet and moving enough until the sun came back to rescue me.

To pluck me from these depths and hopefully, hopefully give me a chance to give the final hours the very best I had within me.

Finally, the dawn light began to creep up – and with it I committed to pushing as hard as my weakened frame would allow. I drove forward like a man possessed, pushing hard off my poles and power walking as fast as I could turn my legs over. In my mind, Patrick was lurking just behind me over that last hill, I had a deep, gut-wrenching fear that if I turned around I would see his figure in the distance and I would know that it was over. I think the sight of him would have broken me on the spot. I allowed myself the very occasional furtive glance and saw nothing behind me but open expanse – devoid of Patrick, devoid of vegetation, devoid of everything but white, hard-packed trail and sky.

With the return of the sun came the hills – climb after climb heading into Tuk. With roughly 30km to go I saw a support crew vehicle coming towards me – it slowed to a stop and Martin got out and walked over to me. I remember what he said with great clarity, 'I'm going to say to you exactly what I'm going to go and say to Patrick – this will come down to minutes. It will come down to mere minutes so you do whatever you feel you need to do. That's all I'm going to say.'

And he drove off.

Patrick must be within about five hours of my position. Apply his time credit and he must be pretty much right on my tail.

I have 30km to go.

They will be hilly.

No matter what, I will hit the finish line on this day – the nights are over.

This will be played out in daylight.

After he drove off – I stopped and stood still. I asked myself a single question. I asked it aloud.

'How bad do you want it?'

The answer was a hammer blow. It held an intensity of the order of my love for my wife and two children. There was nothing more foundational than the answer to that question – I would drive myself to the very edge of my existence to get over that line in enough time to win. No regard for pain or damage or limits or feelings – as long as I lived to see another day I cared not what state I would be in. I would burn my soul to the ground before I gave up and let this slip from my grasp.

And with that decision I started doing something that I had not done in all of the previous 580km – I picked up my poles, loosened my harness and started to run.

After a few kilometres I got a stroke of luck – I had kept my phone tucked away in a pocket under most of my layers so that it not only stayed warm, but I could access it to grab a quick photo or video. Now – all of a sudden – it wanted to make its presence known – it let out a single ping. I have no idea what app or action caused it to make that noise but I had two realisations instantly. First – I must have reception, most likely from Tuk, secondly – I could access the internet.

I stopped and grabbed my phone out – I had only one thing to do and I had to be quick. Once the phone was exposed to the outside air, which was around -21c, the battery would drop from 100% to 0% in literally a minute. I accessed the internet, headed for the GPS tracker link that everyone at home was using to see where all the competitors were on the trail – distance, speed, location. For the first time since leaving Inuvik two days ago I was about to pinpoint Patrick's location exactly.

With just a few percent left on my phone, the page loaded and I spotted it. Patrick was 19.3km behind me. I needed a five-hour buffer – and even that was cutting it so fine as to be almost unimaginably close. We had both been averaging about 5km per hour, 24 hours a day, for the last few days. That gave me four hours if he held that pace. It wasn't enough.

I had the best part of 30km to stretch that lead out as far as possible. A lead of 24 km would be the least I could possibly hope to win with. I couldn't just match his pace, I had to be much faster than he was. Significantly faster. I had to dig even deeper. I felt like a man at the very bottom of a dry well, madly scratching into the bedrock with nothing more than ragged fingernails in a last ditch effort to find water. I had to get mad. I had to get angry. I needed righteous rage and indignation to help me squeeze every last drop out of my exhausted and deeply depleted frame.

But how? What's there to hate? To anger? I cycled through possibilities – he's trying to steal the win from you...no he's not, he's just trying as hard as you are to win. He wants to see you fail... no he doesn't, he's been nothing but decent and honourable and friendly. Hard to get angry at someone when your default nature is the opposite of that, and the person you are focusing on is a just a really nice guy.

Then I found it.

If he beats you – he will deny your two boys the chance to see their Dad succeed, to risk it all and win. He will take that lesson from them.

For the record I know that Patrick never thought any of these things for a second. But I had to suspend reasonable belief for the next few hours to exist in an imaginary world where he was 'trying' to take something from my two boys. I don't care what you think of me but try to deny something of that much importance from my boys, my entire world, then we sir, are going to have a problem.

I ran. I could feel the blisters on both my feet splitting and exploding, the raw flesh beneath being torn apart. I didn't care. A deep split had developed on the bone-dry sole of my right foot a few days ago – I had been cramming it full of Chapstick (the only 'moisturiser' I had) but now it was splitting wide open, rent deep into the raw flesh. So be it.

My back had been progressively tightening and then seizing up for days. Now it had reached a point where the muscular tension was so great it cut off any nerve transmission. The entire surface layer of my back had gone numb – like it had gone to sleep. But underneath the deeper layers were on fire. No matter how I tried to release it or manipulate it or stretch it, it was agony. In the end the only way I could lessen the pain was to put my walking poles together, sling them across my shoulders and lift my hands to hold the two ends, like holding and carrying a yoke. It took just enough pressure off.

So with poles slung across my shoulders, I 'ran'. I ran anything that wasn't a serious climb and power walked as hard as I could on anything that was. The kilometres seemed to inch by. Despite the temperature, around -20C, I started stripping off my many layers – my core temperature was climbing and climbing and now I was starting to sweat. The golden rule had been 'don't sweat' as it left you in a suit of frozen water – an almost guaranteed trigger for hypothermia. Now I didn't care – I knew as soon as I reached the finish line I would be able to retreat into the safety of the local school gymnasium we used as a staging point. The risk was minimal so I took it.

Twenty-two kilometres of climb after climb, sweeping rise after sweeping rise. Finally I reached the plateau that would run me into Tuk. I had approximately eight kilometres to go. I grabbed my phone – the heat of my body had been sufficient to warm it and the battery was working again. I checked the GPS tracker site. The gap between us had grown from 19.3km to 27.3. Not only did Patrick have to push through all the hills that I had just done, but he would have to do it at a pace far above anything he had done in the last eight days. At his average of about 5km per hour I had hopefully put between five and six hours between us.

I stashed my phone again and looked up to see a figure riding out to me on a push bike, fully kitted out for Arctic travel. It was Pete Newland. Just the sight of him lifted my spirits. Pete and I had both competed in 2017 and had both pulled out, at different stages. We had stayed in contact post-race and often talked about pending adventures. He had come back in 2018 and successfully completed the race and been generous with his experience, tips and information in my lead up to 2019. This year he had returned and rode a bike from Whitehorse to Tuk and timed it to meet us all at the finish line. He had ridden almost 1800km in the weeks just gone.

He rode up beside me, 'Mate, this is flippin' brilliant! You're going to bloody win it!'

I have an enormous amount of respect for Pete and to see his genuine excitement at my efforts thus far meant the world. I stopped running and power walked – it gave me the chance to walk with him as we crept closer to the buildings of Tuk. We chatted in the sun and wound our way into town – it was a long road, the road sign welcoming us to Tuk, like all the signs up here, seemed to have been placed about ten kilometres too early. The road went on and on.

I kept a solid pace until we passed a support vehicle with Martin in it – he leant out and frantically indicated that the clock was ticking and Patrick was moving – get going!

Pete smiled and said he would ride ahead to the finish line, only about a kilometre away. He then said something, just a quiet piece of advice and I'll never forget it. I'll ride on ahead and clear the road he said, so you can be alone, have some good thoughts mate about what you've done. This is it. Go finish it.

I crossed the finish line at 2:15pm, Friday. One hundred and ninety five hours and 41 minutes after I had started, 614km away.

I had run the final kilometre. For two days, I had thought about this moment. In truth I had thought about it for almost two years – firstly when I was here in 2017 and then all through my training for 2019. But that had been about finishing, for the last two days it had been about more than that – it had been about winning. In those two days, the very thought of it had brought tears to my eyes, a mixture of emotion, exhaustion, the knowledge that I had delivered the very best execution of a training and race plan that I could possibly imagine. The discipline, the dedication, the pain, the sacrifices, the doubt, the fear, the drive, all of it distilled down to these final moments. I'd thought that crossing that line I would either completely collapse or simply explode. Neither happened.

I rounded the final turn as the gathered support crew, withdrawn athletes, media and medics cheered me on – the finish line is literally at the 'Arctic Ocean' sign – there is no more land to cover. I raised my hands and pushed into the banner.

There was relief but not the emotion or intensity of feelings that I had expected. I think it was due in part to the fact that my mind knew it wasn't over – I'd finished but for four hours and forty seven more minutes I wouldn't know the final outcome. I also think it was sheer exhaustion. I had driven my body through depths and into extremes that even I barely comprehended. I was just empty.

The banner was held up by the other two Australians who had competed but withdrawn – Bronwyn and Matt. Having some fellow Aussies hold that banner as I crossed felt almost poetic and brought a smile to my weary face. After a whirlwind of hugs and congratulations from all directions I turned into a wall of waiting media. I don't know if it's just my dim recollection or not but it seemed as if the cameras pointed but I heard very few questions. In some ways I wasn't sure what to answer – I couldn't say I had won because I hadn't, I couldn't say I didn't win because I might. It was good to be finished and I couldn't wait to get home to my wife and sons. I think that's all I got out.

Thankfully at that point, Jonny the medic pushed through and said he needed me in the car for a check-up, which turned out to be code for let's get you out of here and find some food.

'What do you want to eat?' he asked

'I need a Coke and some fast food,' I replied

I just wanted some calories and a drink that wasn't part of a freeze-dried meal or had the slight flavour of winter mix gas through it.

'I got you covered.' He drove us a few blocks and stopped outside a nondescript building. I suddenly realised I didn't have any money on me – Jonny just laughed,

'Just stay in the car – I'll be back with some serious chicken and chips.'

Sure enough, he did. Two cans of Coke and a box of good old fashioned deep fried chips and chicken breasts. All an exhausted and depleted body needs! A short drive and we were at the Tuktoyaktuk school – they had kindly given us the use of their gymnasium for the few days as the race drew to a close. I slowly walked up the entrance ramp and walked into the gym to find my sled had arrived via other means and was waiting for me.

And wait we did.

CHAPTER 19
Full circle

Tuktoyaktuk.
Northwest Territories, Canada
March, 2019

THE GYMNASIUM WAS BIG BUT BUSY – everyone was here with the exception of the five athletes still out on the trail. So all the support crew, medics, media, withdrawn athletes were bunkered down here. Mats and sleeping bags littered the floor, contents of sled bags were strewn around as people had made themselves at home for the few days that they would spend here.

I gently took off my shoes (no footwear inside) and winced as the raw exposed flesh under my shredded blisters made its presence known. I found a spot and set out my bivvy and dug out my first aid kit, my Tuk drop bag (with a clean set of clothes and a massive Kit Kat bar) and headed into the gym change rooms and bathroom. Good news – there's showers, bad news – cold water only. So the shower can wait till we are back in a hotel, hopefully tomorrow night. I cleaned my teeth – which was nothing short of amazing and had a 'shower' with antiseptic wipes in the toilet. I was thin, despite eating close to 6000 calories per day, pretty much all semblance of body fat had been incinerated over the preceding week. My face was swollen, probably part from exposure, part from sleep deprivation, part systemic inflammation.

I made my way back out into the general area and sat down to finally tuck into my Coke and chicken and chips. From a nutritional standpoint I'm pretty sure it had no redeeming features in terms of being restorative for my body but the sugar would keep me standing for another four hours and 47 minutes, which was all that mattered, and the salty, greasy chips were nothing short of biblical in their magnificence.

It was amazing to finally sit down and catch up with the other athletes, some of them I had competed with in 2017 so we had developed real friendships and shared experience in this hostile environment. To be able to relax and talk was incredible. But I was still in no-man's land. Not a winner, not not a winner. I watched the clock and the GPS tracker site to see how close it would be – and it was going to be close.

Martin no doubt saw my concern, he came over at one point to have a chat – he pointed out that to win Patrick had to hold a pace of 6.4 kilometres per hour for over four hours, that doesn't sound like a fast pace but keep in mind – that's uphill, dragging a sled after racing for 191 hours. Martin felt that that achievement was probably beyond anyone – I pointed out that doing more than 6.4 kilometres per hour for over four hours, uphill, dragging a sled, after racing for 191 hours was exactly what I had just done. If I could do it, so could Patrick.

I started to prepare myself for the 'loss'. Which is a ridiculous term – I simply wouldn't be first, I would still come second in one of the toughest ultra's on the planet. But mentally and emotionally that's where I was. The thought of second place sat like a lead weight deep in my gut. The rational part of me knew I had nothing to be ashamed of or disappointed about but I couldn't help it.

I was sitting at a table eating Pringles and just staring at the clock on the wall. Martin looked at his watch, and calmly leant over and said, 'Congratulations, you are officially the winner.'

I remember smiling but I was almost numb. Part of me was desperately trying to soak up the moment, part of me was collapsing with the knowledge that it was truly over, part of me felt for Patrick – I knew he was out there pushing as hard as I had, I have enormous respect for him and know that his presence drove me to perform at the level I did.

I grabbed my phone and headed out into a hallway to ring my wife, Ilona, and then my parents. As I walked through, I was met with hearty congratulations, handshakes and hugs – that helped cement the fact that it was over and I had won. To be honest it felt far more a victory over myself and the conditions than it did over anyone else. I tucked myself away in the corner of a long hall – sat down under school children's drawings of bears, caribou and Inuit.

When Ilona answered the phone I resorted (as I normally do with her) to my usual humour and total lack of humility, 'Turns out you married a champion…'

She laughed – as she normally does with me. I have no idea how long we spoke for, I know there was laughter, tears and the deep comfort of hearing the voice of the woman you love for the first time in what seems like years. I also rang my parents – long suffering parents who have both watched their wayward son risk life and limb on some of the planet's most remote and unforgiving places for reasons that they – and sometimes I – don't fully understand. Lastly I did a phone interview with a media company from our home town to give some footage and media for friends and followers back home.

When I finally got off the phone and walked back out into the gym I found that everyone was gone. Literally everyone. It took me a moment but then I realised they had all headed out to see Patrick come in and finish – typically everyone will head out to see people cross the finish line regardless of time of day. I was shattered I had missed the chance to see Patrick cross the finish line – I owed him that. And while I missed the chance for the best of reasons, I still regret not being there. I stayed by the front door of the school so I could see him as soon as he came in. When he did arrive, we embraced and congratulated each other – he was drenched, I guessed from sweat – as he had no doubt pushed just as hard as I had. He looked, well he looked about as good as I did when I stumbled into the gym. As good as anyone can look after the ordeal we had put ourselves through.

Over the course of the night and into the early hours of Friday morning, the remaining athletes came in. Avram, David, Hayley and Mark. Finishing the full distance in the time limit is an incredible achievement – the race has an attrition rate of 80%, some years that has been as high as 100%. To finish, regardless of place, is a monumental achievement.

After Patrick had come in, I decided to grab a few hours sleep before heading out to see the next athletes come in. When I awoke, hours later, the last two athletes – Hayley and Mark – had just arrived at the gym. I had either managed to sleep so deeply that no one could wake me or they decided to leave me be. The hours of sleep on the hard wooden gym floor had not been kind. And my body, perhaps realising that the ordeal was over, was now beginning to make abundantly clear how unhappy it was with the previous eight days' shenanigans. Getting up and out of my sleeping bag – a thirty second act on the trail – was now slow and painful. Even walking to the toilet was excruciating, I would manage a few steps and stop, steady myself and move on. Slowly I got the legs and feet to start agreeing and we could get moving. With the arrival of the final athletes, the time had come to pack up, load up and start the long two-day drive back down to Whitehorse. The prospect of spending up to ten hours a day, for the next two days, packed into vehicles was not overly exciting – from a recovery standpoint this was definitely going to hinder, not help.

On the drive up I had been jammed up in the rear seats – pretty much the smallest space in the entire car. I had done so by choice; I was the smallest so it seemed fair. Now I decided to see if my 'winner' status would afford me some privilege and quietly popped myself into the front passenger seat. There were no complaints (that I heard) from the crew behind, so I settled in, turned on the seat heater to try and give my back any form of relief. And so began the long drive.

While physically it was torment being cramped up, it gave my mind some much needed time to process, to try and grasp what had happened, what it meant. In some ways I felt a great sadness as we drove the long miles down the Klondike, Dempster and Alaskan highways. This was it, there would be no need for me to return, the journey here was drawing to its conclusion. There was every chance I would not step foot on this part of the planet again, especially not in these circumstances. There was time to reflect not just on this year but on my attempt in 2017, to try to counterbalance the weight of my 'failure' in 2017 against the achievements and highs of 2019. How did I feel? What did it mean? Did it mean anything? How was I changed? Where do we go from here?

Here's what I posted on Instagram, it's probably the best description of my feelings as it was raw, honest and written in that very moment.

'…Over the last two years the Yukon and Northwest Territories have lead me on a merry dance. It has shown me breathtaking beauty, humbled me with its sheer magnitude, the raw physicality of the weather and brought me to my knees, heartbroken with crushing failure. It has literally flayed the flesh from my bones and left deep marks on my soul.

…But it also had me yelling to Ilona in the middle of the night under bright streams of the northern lights, yelling, 'We're going to make it!' with tears streaming down my face.

It has drained me to the depths and now has filled me back up, made me whole again and sends me home irrevocably changed – in ways that even I'm yet to understand…'

The drive itself was relatively uneventful with one notable exception. The infamous Wrights Pass seemed to want to remind us, for one last time, that we were very much, not in charge. As we crossed the top of the pass the katabatic winds arrived in force, driving huge drifts of snow across the road. The dark path of the road before us vanished in an instant, suddenly the landscape was a seething, roiling white blanket in all directions. The road ceased to exist and the winds slammed into the huge trailer behind us. Joe (a Yukoner) skilfully handled the big vehicle and whip-sawing trailer but eventually the Pass got its way, we were buried deep in a drift. It took twenty minutes of digging and shovelling snow (mainly by hand – we discovered there was only one shovel buried in the trailer) to give us enough clearance. Finally we were on our way again. As we pulled into Eagle Plains, the roads authority were closing the gates that shut the road to all traffic – it had been deemed impassable. Had we been even half an hour later we would have experienced first-hand just how impassable it would become, and we would have found ourselves literally stranded in the car, on the Pass for at least twenty four hours.

Eagle Plains Hotel meant a real feed, a bed and a shower – even if it wasn't overly warm and water 'pressure' was a relative term. I got out of the shower and was finally able to get a look at my body in the mirror. I was thin. I had arrived on the start line weighing in at approximately 71kg. Based on my body weight when I got home a few days later I estimated I had lost between eight and ten kilograms while racing. Even with a 'diet' of 6000 calories per day, my body weight had plummeted. On the plus side, at the age of 43 I finally had a six pack! I tucked into a massive club sandwich, chips and gravy and a few Yukon Gold ales to begin the 'rebuilding' process. Last but not least, I was looking forward to the first full night's sleep in a real bed in ten days. I was to be sorely disappointed.

It wasn't the bed, it was fine. It wasn't noise, or room temperature or even a snoring roommate. It was biochemistry. The medics had given those of us who had completed the entire race fair warning – you probably won't get a good night's sleep for a week or more. Biochemically you are so out of balance, it will be some time before an equilibrium is re-established and some normality can return. Exhausted, depleted and inflamed muscles, aggravated and shortened connective tissues and the bone-deep ache of a body bereft of any homeostasis all conspire to deny you that sleep you feel you so richly deserve. Every few hours I would wake up in a hot sweat, soaked, panicking, thinking I was still in my harness and needed to get up and race. My legs would shake and cramp. My back would seize and generally threaten mutiny whenever I moved. My long held dream of a real sleep was very short lived. It would be eight nights of this before I would finally claim a full and restful night's sleep. The human body truly is a remarkably tough but delicately balanced machine. We can drive it to achieve all manner of amazing feats, but sooner or later a price must be paid. This sleep 're-acclimation' was obviously part of that transaction.

The next day saw the long final drive into Whitehorse. In our absence the temperatures had risen and the snow that had greeted us in Whitehorse was now all but gone. In its place only mud and water. Back into our hotel rooms, gear strewn about on the floor as we all cleaned, sorted and repacked for the long flights home. It was a fairly quiet and reflective time for everyone, I took advantage of some time to go for a few short walks to keep the body moving, as well as some lunches out on my own. Despite having spent so much time alone I still felt the need to almost decompress before diving back into full blown social normality. The world suddenly seemed very loud to me. While the thought of holding my two boys and my wife in my arms again seemed dreamlike, the rest of the world seemed to have a faulty volume dial, stuck way above any necessary or reasonable threshold.

The night before most of us flew out there was a group dinner and trophy presentation. Everyone gets a small trophy, regardless of finishing the full distance or not. Third and second place get larger ones and the outright winner gets the main trophy. I have an extremely clear recollection of this ceremony from 2017, going up to get my little trophy and shaking Martin's hand. I knew that, 'it was an achievement just to get to the start line', and that I'd covered almost 250km and was one of the last to pull out, but it all felt undeserved and unfinished to me, I didn't realise just how deep those feelings ran at the time but they made themselves known in the weeks and months that followed. As I shook Martin's hand in 2017, a line came through my head – I'm honestly not sure if I said it aloud or if it was internal, but it was not premeditated, it arrived unannounced, 'I'll see you in the hills'. Some part of me knew then that I would be back.

Trophies were handed out, speeches were made and finally it was my time to stand. Martin gave me the man hug to end all man hugs. He's a vigorous hugger our Martin, but he's passionate about his race and the people that face it. I made a very short speech. It was from the heart and off-the-cuff – I feel that is when I speak best, truthfully and with no pretence or preparation.

'...there is really only two things I want to say. Firstly, I often joke about the fact that I say I am a 'nerd' and when I talk to people I say I'm kind of 80% Harry Potter, 20% Bear Grylls, but after this

I feel that I can maybe push that out to 60/40. I think I have earned that. This was definitely unfinished business for me, I remember shaking Martin's hand in 2017 and getting my little trophy and knowing I felt like I hadn't earned it and that I would have to come back to resolve that – and I really feel I have done that now!

'I choose these races not because of the name, no one at home knows of this particular race, but I choose them for the place and really for the people in it. You all make the race – pure and simple. I've made friends here I will cherish for a very, very long time, some very special and unique people that I will hold very dear. So thank you for the opportunity, thank you for sharing the trail with me, it was my absolute pleasure and honour to be here, thank you…'

EPILOGUE

Do you fear the wind?

> 'You are more powerful than you think you are.
> Act accordingly.'
> *Seth Godin, Seth's Blog, 24/6/17*

IN THEIR 2018 BOOK, *The Coddling of the American Mind*, Lukianoff and Haidt presented the three great untruths as they saw them; that what doesn't kill you makes you weaker, that you should always trust your feelings and that life is a battle between good people and evil people. Their hypothesis being that the presentation and peddling of these concepts was weakening a generation and setting the scene for broad scale failure. Super positive stuff…but strangely, anecdotally, this nerdy father from a regional town not only agrees with their premise but has seen his own experience bare them out to be true, even if seen from a different viewpoint. I do believe that healthy hardship is not only good for you but vital. Feelings are indeed a quintessential part of the human experience but we must develop the capacity to see them for what they are and how they are both at times friend and foe. And lastly tribalism is, in my opinion, alive and well. In many cases in the worst way possible.

It's like watching two movies unfold at different speeds. The first, modernity, is moving at an unrelenting and unyielding pace. A high-speed, broadband mega-highway with apparently no Malthusian speed limits. The sky is literally not the limit. Imagine for a moment speaking to someone from a century in our past and trying to explain to them that we now have small hand-sized devices we can carry giving us almost unrestricted access to huge swathes of the entirety of human knowledge, and then telling them we use those devices to throw birds at pigs, post carefully edited pics of what we are doing day to day and to 'listen' to people yelling at other people. I'm not a technophobe or a raving critic of the modern world – I have and use as many gadgets as the next person (and I've thrown the odd angry bird at a pig) but at some point you need to step back and realise that when everyone gets a megaphone, that bias (both imposed and unintentional) becomes rife and that the volume button seems to be stuck on 11. You need to be able to step back and be an island in the stream by choice as opposed to a branch being hurled along by the current.

I'm not advocating that you suddenly take off on some Thoreau-like, Waldenesque adventure. Nor do you need to join the ranks of the Amish or build an apocalypse bunker. What I am advocating is that you need to develop a substantial degree of self-reliance. To garner a position from which you can be selective in what you add to your framework rather than having many of those choices made for you, often without your conscious knowledge or understanding.

The second and slower movie, is evolution. Why is it not that difficult to split people into tribes? Because we have been wired that way for a very long time. A very long time. Originally it was about survival, unfortunately today it seems much more about division and the labelling of right and wrong and therefore, often, good or evil. Your body and brain are moving at one pace trying to adapt and adjust to its surroundings and experiences, but it is doing so at a pace far slower than the speed with which the world around is changing. Good news is you can reach back into some of those evolutionary embedded traits and use them to augment your capacity to thrive in a modern world.

Even better – you don't need to spend any money – you already have everything you need.

Drop the labels.

No one expects the nerdy Dad to win. For a long time, neither did the nerdy Dad. We are very fast to label ourselves and suddenly yield under the yoke of all the burdens that come with those self-ascribed labels. That's on you. So the answer is on you too. Start seeing yourself for your story and not your business card title or the day-to-day reality of you in this instant. You are not an architect, or plumber, or stay-at-home parent, you are far more. You are the victories, failures, adventures, experiences, skills and abilities that fill all your hours, days, months and years. Do not get sucked into playing the game whereby your political affiliation, job title or salary cap allow others to pigeonhole you and box you up. You have to take those labels off yourself and in doing so give yourself the freedom to do…anything. *I shouldn't do that* or *can't do that* because that's not me, or *people like me don't do that*, or *can't do that*.

What if you *were* that person, what if you *could* do that? As Les Brown says, 'It's your movie, you're the director, you wrote the script.' So write your own script – and realise that now is just a scene, or an episode, in a much bigger season. So build for the big story, rather than getting lost in the trappings of a single episode.

Do the work.

Mental, physical, emotional fortitude. These are the greatest tools you can craft, the greatest gifts you can bestow. In all three cases the secret lies in doing the work required to build them. There are no shortcuts here, no pill, no cheat sheet, no outsourcing. Good news is that it can be summed up as a one-step plan. You have to do the work. And while the work often looks rather uncomfortable and unpleasant, rest assured you are more than capable to doing it. Trust me – you're both waterproof and windproof. Your body is a magnificent machine and even if it doesn't seem overly robust right now, it will respond to imposed demand and deliver. But you have to give it the chance – in general terms that means doing all that stuff that your parents berated you about – eat your greens, go to bed early, get outside and work/play.

If this all sounds a little daunting and a lot like hard work (which it is) the silver lining is that you don't have to look at these as three separate tasks – mental, emotional and physical. It is virtually impossible to train any in isolation, if you are working on one you are simultaneously working on at least one if not two more.

Make incremental change and play the long game. Don't read this book and suddenly go out and try to drag a tyre for ten kilometres and then live off kale and steamed chicken breast for a week – that will not end well. Remember – your story is vast, so don't try to pack the entire script into a week, or a month or even a year. Set your alarm and get up two minutes earlier every day for the next month – and have the discipline to do it – seriously, if you can't get up a measly two minutes earlier than planned there are some bigger issues at hand. Do that for a month and then stick at that point – you just found an extra hour in your day, an extra seven hours per week. Apply that logic to anything – compound interest for the win. Make it small so it's almost inexcusable not to do it and then stay the course.

Learn to be ok on your own – physically, mentally, emotionally. To steal from Picasso, 'without great solitude, no serious work is possible'. Take personal responsibility for your capacity, be strong enough and athletic enough to manage most things that may come your way. You don't have to be Thor or The Mountain but I am yet to find a negative to being relatively robust. Know how to treat and manage your body in basic terms, you should be able to change a tyre just as much as you should know how to unglue your hips and or turn your glutes on if your lower back is complaining. Be aware of what you are – a functioning human being – and the basic tenets of how you work, and then leverage that. Find some alone time – not to ponder and solve the mysteries of the universe, but to simply turn the volume dial down as low as possible for a while. Some may go for a run, do yoga, walk the dog, go camping, fishing, have a cup of tea on the porch, whatever it is – but do it in silence, don't multi-task and don't try to 'win' at meditation. Just learn to be still.

Go hungry and cold like the wolf.

Get uncomfortable from time to time. Leave the comfort zone behind and challenge yourself. Tap into some of that primordial spark bubbling away deep inside and give it a positive and rewarding voice. It is in there whether you acknowledge it or not, and for some it will eat away at them as they try to reconcile modern human with the lost savage one within. Feel the slash of the rain, the force of the wind. Go hungry. Get cold. I mean all of these things in the literal sense – I'm not even being metaphoric. It will make you a better human if you can learn to face these things and realise that if you remain in control, they are not to be avoided but embraced from time to time.

Do the work and learn to love it, to revel in it, to command it rather than be burdened by it. It is not enough to simply trudge ahead simply existing day after day – you need to imagine Sisyphus happy. Revel in your capacity. The final step is in realising that by becoming a better human yourself, you then bring all your renewed spark to those who truly matter, outside of yourself – family, children, loved ones, friends.

POST SCRIPT
What Happened Next

One of the advantages of getting your hands on the updated, second print run edition of this book is that I've had a chance to update the story for you. We can actually answer the question - what happened next?

For some time, nothing at all. The twin troubles of COVID as well as not really being sure what I wanted to do next held all the plans at bay. Winning the 6633 had opened all manner of doors and I had some very exciting plans and schemes floated across the desk.

In the end it boiled back down to that question of - what do I actually want? So we return to the rules - find something that lights the fires and sit on it for thirty days. Then hit question two - if you could do it and no one would know and you could never tell a soul - do you still want to do it? And sure enough - an adventure came along that fit the bill.

As a scientist a question had been nibbling away at me - was my process for the 6633 and subsequent win repeatable? Had I developed a map that would allow me to 'rinse and repeat' and produce a similar outcome. Or had I just been 'lucky'?

All of that saw me eventually sign up and hand over my hard earned money to secure a spot on the starting line of the 2023 Montane Lapland Arctic Ultra (MLAU).

The MLAU is 500km of single stage, self supported Arctic Ultra goodness across Europe's last great wilderness - the Laplandian Arctic in northern Sweden.

A case of same, same, but different compared to the 6633 - same Arctic environment but no roads, all backcountry snow mobile trails, lake crossings and snow laden forests. Checkpoint cabins perched on hill tops or tucked away in the midst of tiny villages hidden in wintery white.

I prepared and planned based on one premise - can I repeat an outcome? I went there to win. It's a very different mindset to both prep and then attempt to execute with the narrow margin of 'success' defined by a spot on the podium.

Needless to say, things didn't exactly go to plan. Well, not entirely. Eight cold, hard days, 500km and over 750,000 steps later and I'd learnt a great deal. But that's a story for another book...

(If you can't wait - you can read my race report from the MLAU on my blog www.paulwatkins.com.au/blog)

THANK YOU

Based purely on the time it takes, I sometimes feel that the simple act of stopping and reading a book is both a luxurious and rebellious act. So thank you for taking the time out of your own life to take a peek into mine. I hope that both my successes and failures have given you not only pause for thought and perchance to dream, but maybe a laugh and a smile at my expense as well.

You can find the background on a number of my other expeditions and business adventures at www.paulwatkins.com.au – as well as on Instagram @the.rogue.scholar. Feel free to reach out and connect via either medium whether it's to discuss speaking engagements or for advice on how to repair frozen wheel bearings on your sled at 3am when it's -36C and the nearest hardware store is almost 200km away.

www.ingramcontent.com/pod-product-compliance
Lightning Source LLC
Chambersburg PA
CBHW051421290426
44109CB00016B/1380